"THIS INTRIGUING AND THOUGHT-PROVOKING BOOK IS FOR THE SKEPTIC AS WELL AS THE BELIEVER . . ."

—SUSAN STRASBERG

Gently I held my palms over his lower back, directly over the scars left by his operation. I felt an intense desire to help relieve my father's pain . . . When over the next few weeks we realized my father's relief was going to last, our amazement gave way to joy. It was then that I began to understand and accept what I had done. My journey into a new way of life had begun . . .

PORTRAIT OF A PSYCHIC HEALER

Dean Kraft

BERKLEY BOOKS, NEW YORK

This Berkley book contains the complete
text of the original hardcover edition.
It has been completely reset in a type face
designed for easy reading, and was printed
from new film.

PORTRAIT OF A PSYCHIC HEALER

A Berkley Book / published by arrangement with
G. P. Putnam's Sons

PRINTING HISTORY
G. P. Putnam's Sons edition / July 1981
Berkley edition / December 1982

ISBN: 0-425-05664-3

Acknowledgments

Many people have given me assistance, encouragement, and support during the writing of this book. I could not have completed the project without them, and to these people I express my love and thanks.

I am grateful to Denise Demong for her invaluable assistance in the preparation of the manuscript, and to Elisabeth Jakab, my editor, for her early insight and open-mindedness and her strong belief in the project.

I also want to thank Abraham and Gertrude Kraft, the most understanding, supportive, and loving parents anyone could ever be blessed with; my sisters, Roberta and Lisa, for their continued love and understanding, and my brothers-in-law, Harvey J. Levine and Norman Kubie.

The longtime love, support, and extraordinary friendship of Dr. Marcy and Mimi Goldstein, Bob and Candace Williamson, and Drs. Maxine Haft and Howard White also helped make this book possible.

There are many more additional friends and relatives to whom I owe great thanks than I could ever list. But special gratitude goes to Steve Axelrod,

Irma and Burt Bacharach, Kitty Benedict, Michael Brown, Bill and Kay Church, Ken Cooper, Dr. Erwin DiCyan, Dr. Louis and Deanna Elias, Marilyn Englese, Albert Z. Freedman, Jack Freedman, Maureen and Mort Gale, Buddy and Shirley Geier, David and Florence Gromadzin, Fred Gromadzin, Mark and Jeannie Gromadzin, Dr. Hans Holzer, Dr. Gerald Jampolsky, Maria and Byron Janis, Dr. John M. Kmetz, Helen Kruger, Dr. David Laskowitz, Judge Isidore and Annette Levine, Detective H. John McGrath, Yoko Ono and the late John Lennon, Nancy Perlman, Robert Perrin, Don Schlessel, Henry C. Shays, Marvin and Sue Sheinis, Pauline and Harry Sheinis, Paul Silverman, Judith R. and Robert Skutch, Sam Sunshine, and Joseph Wagner.

Without the perseverance, sacrifice, and support of my loving wife, Rochelle, this book would still be a fantasy.

Because of her remarkable writing skill and her constant inspiration, I truly consider her my coauthor and humbly dedicate this book to her with all my love.

Contents

Author's Note

Most of the names and identities in this book are real, and, where appropriate, permission to use them has been granted. In a few instances—as, for example, in the case of an individual who is no longer alive or could not be located, or when anonymity has been requested—fictitious names have been assigned. Their use is indicated in the text. In all cases, histories and documentation are on file with the author.

PORTRAIT OF A PSYCHIC HEALER

1.

Healing: A New Way of Life

I cannot recall a day when I was growing up that my father's back didn't hurt him or make him cry out in pain as he turned in his sleep.

His trouble had begun during the Second World War, when he fell while lifting heavy antiaircraft equipment and ruptured a disc in his back. That injury went undiagnosed for three years before surgery was performed. Severe back and neck pains plagued Dad thereafter, and eventually he was diagnosed as having a rare form of osteoarthritis called Marie-Strümpell disease.

My father was robbed of his mobility. As he described it, every move sent searing pokers of pain through his body. It usually took him two hours in the morning to wash and dress himself. When I was little it was difficult for him to get down on the floor and play with me, as fathers usually do with their sons. He would do it anyway, but slowly, awkwardly.

1

Even today, my father has only a touch of gray in his thick, dark, wavy hair, but fifteen years ago he looked and moved like an old man. He's short to begin with, and during the late sixties his back became increasingly hunched because of growing calcium buildup along his spine. He had a closetful of corsets and back braces, but in time he found it difficult to walk, even with a cane. Still, my father is a very positive man, and he never complained to Mom, my sisters, or me. When the pain really got to my father I could see the sadness in his eyes. He'd get very tired, and he'd often lie down or even sleep. When his pain was less, he'd cover it up. He hid his pain a lot.

One cold Monday night in 1974, when I was twenty-four, I woke up to hear my father yelling in his sleep. For what seemed like the first time, I really thought about his suffering. I guess that up till then I'd taken his illness as a given—he'd been sick as long as I could remember. But just days before, I had tried, for the first time consciously, to heal. I had laid my hands upon my brother-in-law's head and apparently relieved him of the pain of his migraine. Now I wondered, was it possible I could do something to help my father?

It was on the day when I had apparently healed my brother-in-law that I first shared with my parents the strange string of experiences that had shaken my life in recent years. Incredible though it was, I seemed to have acquired some strange power—a power to move objects with my mind, to see events at a distance, and now, it seemed, even to heal. My parents were still reeling from this extraordinary revelation, but when I asked my father how he felt about my trying to use the strange energy I was apparently able to harness to help him, he agreed readily. "Let's try it," he said.

My father is not a flighty man. If he hadn't seen me move objects without touching them I'm sure he would have sent me to a psychiatrist for claiming to do so. But my father knew me well enough to know when I was serious, and he knew I'd never been interested in psychic events or played with magic. During the past few days he had seen me do remarkable things, and since he had tried just about everything to get relief from his pain, including all the treatments offered by conventional medicine, and even acupuncture, he was more than willing to be my guinea pig.

My mother also thought it was a terrific idea for me to work on Dad and seemed optimistic that I might be able to help him in some way. I didn't know what to expect. I regarded my attempt as an experiment to satisfy my curiosity about my healing abilities. I knew how wonderful it would be if my father found some relief, but I felt no pressure to succeed. I had no fear of failure, for I wasn't really attached to the idea that I might have a true healing ability.

I led my father into the den of our four-room Brooklyn apartment and asked him to straddle a straight-backed chair. He took off his shirt, showed me his scars, pointed out the different areas of discomfort and told me in some detail how his back condition had developed, much as he might have explained it to a doctor. I'd understood his illness only vaguely before.

Then I stood behind Dad, closed my eyes and began to breathe deeply and slowly. Gently I put my palms next to his lower back, about half an inch from his skin, directly over the scars left by his operations.

I can still remember the sudden and tremendous feeling of warmth, of oneness, that overwhelmed me. I felt an intense desire to help relieve my father's pain, to give of myself to him. It was an overpowering sense of love. This was my first realization that healing is love, as corny as it sounded, even to me.

As soon as I placed my hands near my father's back I felt a response, a movement that told me he felt something. When I opened my eyes to glance at him, he wore a look of contentment. I felt a loosening of his body; he seemed to relax into the chair.

Just as when I had worked with my brother-in-law, I felt a warm, tingling sensation running through my body. In my mind's eye I saw some kind of energy, vibrating like heat waves above a hot street, penetrating the skin of my father's back and surrounding what seemed to look like inflamed muscles, displaced vertebrae, and sharp points of accumulated calcium deposits. It wasn't that I had any medical knowledge; my visualization grew from what we all know of the human body and from what my father had described to me. I felt like an observer; my mind seemed to lay out a map indicating where my hands were to proceed next. At one point, hearing a rustling in the room, I opened my eyes a crack to see my mother dusting the table near the couch, no longer watching the interaction between my father and me. Closing my eyes again, I chuckled, for I knew how hard it was for mother to sit still for any length of time. As I continued the treatment I noted with surprise that I had never lost track of the visualization in my mind.

For perhaps twenty minutes I concentrated on releasing energy, and then I felt intuitively that the session was complete. Anxiously I walked around the chair to face my father. He started to turn his body at different angles. He looked surprised, and I could see that he was impressed. "I really felt something!" he exclaimed over and over to my mother. "It felt like an electrical charge was coming form Dean's hands." He could still feel it, along with a soothing warmth. He got up, walked around, twisted his neck and nodded excitedly. The muscle spasms he'd awakened with that morning were gone. He felt no pain!

My father's main reaction that first day was amazement. As for me, I wasn't sure whether to believe him when he said he felt better. I thought maybe he was just saying it to encourage me. I really began to accept the possibility that I had helped him with my hands when my mother told me the next morning that he hadn't cried out once during the night. He had awakened without his usual stiffness and pain, and even his attitude had changed. That morning there were no signs of the subtle depression —caused by his doctor's prediction that eventually he would be immobilized by his disease—that normally underlay my father's every mood.

It was over the next few weeks that we both began to believe that perhaps my father's relief was going to last; amazement gave way to joy. I worked with my father as often as possible between his long hours at work and my own hectic schedule. Soon it became apparent that even with his increased mobility and comfort, his job, where he had to lift heavy boxes, placed a great strain on his heart, so at fifty-nine my father retired. His new freedom meant that I could work with him more often, and within the next few months, the results of my treatment were dramatic. Dad began to hold his back straighter when he walked, and soon he discarded his cane.

When I was growing up, my father's jobs had

demanded so much of his time that we weren't able to be together very much, but I had always felt his affection, for he was an unusually loving parent. He did as well as he could under the circumstances, and family was important to him—I can remember him closing up his grocery store to take my sister to the doctor when she had a virus. A few years ago, after I had become somewhat well known, my father was interviewed by a reporter, and when he began to explain that he'd never been able to spend much time with me he broke down and cried.

After Dad's retirement we began to grow much closer. We were together more often than ever before, and our healing sessions, calm and quiet periods of physical closeness, became the occasions for a new emotional intimacy as well.

A few months after I first tried to heal my father my parents went to their family doctor, because Dad was scheduled for back and chest X rays. They came home with incredible news. The X rays showed that the calcification along his spinal column—the source of his pain—had lessened significantly, and that his spine itself had definitely straightened.

I immediately asked how the doctor had explained the changes, but he had offered no real explanation. Indeed, the doctor was baffled. Although the X rays showed dramatic improvement, Dad still had Marie-Strümpell, yet he was not only standing straight, but no longer complained of the severe pains that normally accompany the disease. The important thing, as far as my father was concerned, was that he felt better than he had in years. I was happy for him, but even after hearing the news I found it hard to believe that my father could have gotten such relief from my hands.

Later that afternoon my father asked me to go fishing with him on the docks at Sheepshead Bay. I was stunned, for my father had always been too uncomfortable to enjoy fishing. I'll never forget watching my father cast a fishing rod that day—it was the first time he had done so in thirty years. Holding the pole up with his arm high above his head, he turned to look at me with a grin, tears welling up in his eyes. He said nothing, just kissed the back of my neck, a loving gesture he had bestowed on me whenever I got a haircut as a kid.

It was then I began to understand and accept what I had done. For the first time I considered the possibility of healing as a serious endeavor. Doubts and questions lingered, but my journey into a new way of life had begun.

2.

My Strange Path to Healing

The impulse to lay my hands on my father's back in an attempt to relieve his pain was the culmination of a series of events that had plunged my life into chaos for the past few years. These events were so bizarre that at times I thought I must be losing my sanity.

Certainly none of the events of my childhood resemble the very strange experiences that many psychics and faith healers can attest to. I was brought up in a middle-class Jewish family. My parents didn't expose us to a particularly strong religious beliefs, and my life was void of any psychic encounters. I was never the least bit interested in healing, spiritualism, or anything else related to the "occult." On the whole, mine was an unremarkable childhood.

My parents had met during World War II in Washington, D.C.; my father had just joined the army and my mother was a clerical worker. After the war they had lived in New York until a job for my father drew them back to Washington in 1950. On

April 14 of that year I was born. Shortly thereafter, my father's independent nature asserted itself, and he decided to go into business for himself, opening a grocery store, Tiny's Market, named for mother, who's under five feet tall.

For a few years my parents, my older sister, Roberta, and I lived over the store. But by 1959 the business was well established, and soon after the birth of my sister Lisa in that year we moved into a large house in Chevy Chase, Maryland, where we lived a pleasant, upper-middle-class existence.

Our carefree days there came to an end in the early 1960s. The pain caused by my father's old injury grew severe, and his illness, with its grim prognosis, was identified. Then a succession of robberies took place around the grocery store. We were all scared, because a couple of other storeowners, friends of ours, were killed. Police were staked out in the back of my father's store for three months. Just thinking about that period I can almost feel the tension that gripped our home.

In 1963 my father sold the store and the house at a tremendous loss, and we moved back to New York, to a three-room garden apartment in Queens. Since we were used to an eight-room house, it was pretty close quarters. To support the family Dad took two jobs, and he rarely got home before midnight. When a better job—managing a cosmetics firm—opened up, we moved to Sheepshead Bay in Brooklyn.

I enjoyed our new neighborhood, where I could go fishing in the bay and play baseball and football at the local playgrounds. But I never liked being a drain on my folks, and at the age of thirteen, feeling the need for more pocket money, I took a job at a dry-cleaning store. A year later I moved to a job as a stockboy at a nearby discount department store.

One of the first things I bought after I started working was an electric guitar, and in time I became proficient enough to lead my own rock group, which played at local dances and clubs. By the time I was sixteen I wanted to be even more involved in the music world, so I moved to an after-school job as a salesman at Buddy's, a music store owned by Buddy Geier. A pleasant, conservative, but happy-go-lucky musician in his mid-fifties, Buddy had played sax for such well-loved leaders as Benny Goodman and Vaughn Monroe during the days of the big bands. From the day he and I met we really hit it off. Despite the difference in our ages we had a great deal in common, and there was enough of a physical resemblance between us that we were often mistaken for father and son.

At Buddy's I quickly learned to play many different musical instruments, because I had to demonstrate them for customers. Rock groups were forever in and out of the store, trading equipment and bits of gossip. We discussed groups, dates, performances —everything in the music field. I was in my element.

In time it occurred to me that it might be possible to act as a link between the two types of customers who frequented Buddy's Music Store: the club owners who came to buy new amplifiers and speakers and the many musicians and groups who I knew were starved for work. I began to act as an agent, suggesting to the club owners groups for them to book at their nightspots. Everyone benefited: the owners got good entertainment; the groups got bookings; Buddy's Music thrived; and I got a ten percent agent's fee. The business began to snowball, and though I had enrolled at Long Island University in political science, college was no longer a priority. In fact, it quickly became a nuisance. My major changed every semester.

The business grew so much that Buddy opened a second store, on West Forty-eighth Street and Seventh Avenue in Manhattan—an area crowded with music stores—and he named me manager. By then my confidence was booming, and my ego was keeping pace. I rearranged the New York store hours to fit my schedule and let one of the salesmen open up in the morning, since my talent business kept me out till all hours. Just before I turned twenty-one I dropped out of college.

Then something happened that entirely changed my life, blotting out all the interests that had kept me busy and satisfied.

In the years since I have often wondered about the incredible turn of events that so drastically altered the lifestyle of a young man from such a "normal" background. But as many times as I have asked myself, "Why me?" I have found no logical or even moderately satisfactory answer.

It was the late fall of 1972. Buddy Geier and I were driving home in his rented 1971 Buick Electra after a hectic day in Manhattan. We had just gotten off the Prospect Expressway onto Ocean Parkway in Brooklyn when all four electric door locks in the car began clicking rapidly up and down. After making sure that neither of us was touching the control buttons, Buddy and I concluded that the clicks must be the result of an electrical short. The locks continued to move up and down every few minutes.

Then Buddy suggested, in fun, that perhaps some spirit was responsible for the clicks. Maybe his deceased mother was trying to communicate with him. So I jokingly commanded, "If there is a spirit in this car, give me five clicks!"

CLICK CLICK CLICK CLICK CLICK

Buddy and I stared at each other aghast. Then, excitedly, we called for more clicks from the car. Whatever was making the door locks move responded correctly to commands for ten and then fifteen clicks. Trying to come up with some rational explanation for what was happening, Buddy and I pulled the car off to the side of the road and turned the engine off, figuring that the door locks should stop moving, since they were electrical. Neither of us quite believed that the other wasn't playing some kind of joke, so, to be sure, we sat in the middle of the seat, holding each other's hands and wrapping our legs across each other. I was just contemplating the possibility of a policeman spotting us like that—"Oh, hi, officer, we're just communicating with spirits"—when Buddy asked, "How much is two plus two?"

Four jumps of the locks immediately answered.

My initial reaction was that Buddy *had* to be playing a trick on me. But when I saw his expression I dismissed the idea. The hair at the nape of his neck was literally curling up. By then I'd known Buddy for several years and in all sorts of situations, even during attempted robberies at the store, but I had never seen him look so frightened. When I stepped out of the car I felt chilled, confused, and anxious.

That night Buddy called to say that the door locks had stopped clicking after he dropped me off. I didn't dare tell my family what we'd experienced, for I was sure they would think I had lost my mind. But I did mention it to Sam Sunshine, a musician who was also a good friend. Sam, a big, quiet, calm guy, got so curious that he joined Buddy and me in the car the next day. We started posing mathematical questions again, and again the door locks clicked in response. After he had checked the car and convinced himself that there was no trickery involved, Sam was as astonished as we were by the accurate response of the clicks. In weeks to come, Buddy's wife, Shirley, and seven other close friends witnessed the eerie communicative clicking of the door locks, which only occurred when I was in the car.

Each time I was about to tell my folks I thought twice about it. It was all too crazy. I hardly believed what was happening myself, but the clicks had happened so many times in front of so many people that we had ruled out mass hysteria and, as best we could, we had ruled out deception. If it hadn't been for all the other witnesses I probably would have committed myself.

All the time our "communication" with the door locks was growing more complex. First we developed a "one-click-for-no, two-clicks-for-yes" code that enabled us to ask simple—and often silly—questions, like "Did we have a good day at the store today?"

Then we figured out an alphabet code: I would ask a question and Buddy would slowly recite the alphabet, stopping whenever we heard a click. Sam, sitting in the back seat armed with a pencil and paper, would write down the letter indicated by the click. Then Buddy would start again from A until we heard another click. Individual letters formed words and sentences. Provided with this new verbal ability, the locks clicked out messages that ranged from the seemingly prophetic—DEAN, YOU WILL HAVE ALL POWERS; USE THEM CAREFULLY—to the more mundane; once when Shirley and Buddy had been quarreling, we deciphered the words, THERE IS NO TIME FOR ARGUING; YOU TWO WORRY TOO MUCH. Often the last message of the evening was GOOD NIGHT.

I kept trying to carry on a normal existence, but it was becoming increasingly difficult, especially in front of my family. Still, every time I thought about the craziness of our sessions in the car, I erased the thought of telling them from my mind.

About a week before Christmas of 1972 I was working in the Buddy's Music Store in Manhattan when I heard the screech of a car, followed by agonized screams. I watched in horror as a young woman, pinned under the low running board of an old car, was dragged down the street. I immediately ran out to help lift the car and free her.

The woman was bleeding profusely and seemed to be in shock. Without thinking I knelt in the crowded street to try to comfort her, gently stroking the hair from her damp forehead. Suddenly I felt a strong, compassionate sensation—I felt a "oneness" with this stranger that I'd never felt before. But before I could think further about it an ambulance arrived, and the attendants quickly removed the woman on a special slat stretcher, for their speedy diagnosis indicated broken bones.

That night, as Buddy and I headed home in this car, the door locks began clicking. No longer surprised at anything that could happen in that car, I quickly grabbed a pen and a piece of paper from the floor as Buddy began reciting the alphabet. The message read: DEAN, YOUR HAND HEALED TODAY. Immediately I looked at my hands for a cut or scratch that might have healed, but I saw nothing, and I couldn't remember hurting myself. The locks clicked a second message: HELP THOSE WHO NEED HELP. Then Buddy suggested that perhaps the "healing" the first message had referred to was connected with the car accident earlier in the day.

The idea seemed preposterous. But we were curious enough to call the hospital the following morning, and we learned that the woman admitted after the car accident had been released with minor cuts and bruises. The thought that I might have had anything to do with it was too big for me to handle. I looked down at my hands—there was nothing striking or unusual about them—and dismissed the thought of strange healing powers immediately. I knew that the woman could have been misdiagnosed by the ambulance attendants on the scene.

My life was becoming an unending adventure. One evening Buddy, Sam, and I were having dinner together in a restaurant in downtown Manhattan, when I suddenly began to feel nauseous and dizzy. Buddy and Sam became quite concerned because, they said, I looked terrible. But I couldn't even speak. All I seemed able to do was to sit in a stupor, staring at the giant woodblock table at which we were sitting.

As I continued to stare I began to feel a tingling all over. Flashes of heat raced through my body. A pounding in my temples began, like a hammer beating inside my head. I found it hard to draw a full breath. I was terrified! Could I be having a heart attack at twenty-two? Then I saw a crazy vision—I saw myself as if from a distance, stretched out on the floor on my stomach, with the base of this large table on my back. I could feel the pressure on my spine, and then I saw myself squirming under the table, trying to shake it off.

Suddenly I felt as though my brain were pulsating; with every breath it seemed as though my head were expanding. Then I felt a sharp pinprick in the center of my forehead, and what seemed to be compressed power that had built up inside of me began to pour out, concentrated on my mental picture of the table on my back. Abruptly the table in front of us started moving, rattling the glasses and dishes. Buddy and Sam jumped away and raised the tablecloth. They saw that no part of my body was touching the table. I was still sitting motionless, staring blankly. Then I felt myself grow faint. The pounding in my temples stopped, my head dropped to my chest, and the table stopped moving.

I still felt dreadfully sick, and I dashed off to the bathroom to splash cold water on my face and neck. That made me feel somewhat better, but a strange sensation remained. Dazed, I rejoined Buddy and Sam and assured them I was all right. Buddy excitedly suggested that what had just happened between the table and me was psychokinesis or PK—the moving of objects by thought alone. It sounded like a lot of nonsense, but there was no denying that the table *had* moved. This on top of the mysterious occurrences in the car! I didn't know what to think anymore.

Wonder and curiosity prompted me to try to recreate the feelings that had overtaken me—and perhaps the effects—voluntarily. Looking discreetly around the restaurant, Buddy, Sam, and I selected as my target a heavy wooden table like ours at which six businessmen were seated. I began to concentrate intensely, imagining as vividly as I could that the table across the room was on my back. Then, in my mind, I tried to shake it off. After a few minutes I saw that the table across the room was beginning to move. This time I was more aware of everything—I could hold on to my visualization and also watch what was going on at the other table. It was quivering so much that the men were shouting at each other, "Hey! Stop playing around! Quit shaking the table!" and looking at each other to find the joker.

The concentration it took for me to move the second table was a great strain. I felt weak, but the excitement I felt in knowing that I had actually moved that object with my mind overshadowed any physical depletion. My friends were speechless; I fixed my sights on coming back to "reality." Reality . . . what was my reality? Buddy and Sam had seen the table move, too—that much was a great relief. But this couldn't really be happening! I felt as if I were entering the Twilight Zone.

I was in for still more. Clairvoyance (literally "clear sight")—the ability to perceive events beyond the range of the five senses—intruded into my increasingly confused world. Coming out of a movie theater in Greenwich Village with Buddy one evening, I suddenly "saw" a blue room and a fire. I had a strong feeling that Buddy should call his wife, who was at their condominium in Miami, Florida, and when he did he learned that there had been a minor fire in their living room that very afternoon. The room was decorated in shades of blue!

I had a similar vision one night a few months later when I was driving on the Belt Parkway in Brooklyn, on my way home from a date. The radio was broken, and I was humming aimlessly, when I suddenly received a mental picture of a fire burning on top of water. Trying to shake this strange image I opened the window to get some fresh air, but the vision of fire on water remained.

In a kind of fog I drove past my exit on the parkway. I had reached Seagate, a private community at the very tip of Brooklyn, when I heard shrill sirens and saw flashing lights as police cars sped down the usually quiet streets.

Driving closer to the shore, I saw a glow on the water—a fire! But how could that be? I stopped a policeman. He explained that two oil barges traveling in opposite directions had collided under the Verrazano-Narrows Bridge. A subsequent explosion had caused the oil spilling on the water to burst into flames. The police needed help in getting survivors out of the freezing waters. As I hurried to the water's edge to join the chain of volunteers a chill ran down my spine. My eerie premonition had come true.

I was still afraid to tell my family about my new "talents." But one evening, while watching my sister Lisa, then fifteen, playing with a Ouija board with a few friends in the apartment, I was seized by the impulse to show off at last. Though I had "played" with my psychokinetic ability at times since the restaurant incident with Buddy and Sam—levitating pencils and such—I had been afraid to push it too far, since I didn't know what I was dealing with.

Lisa and her friends watched in silence as I got into the now familiar deep state of concentration, visualizing a connection between my hands and the Ouija indicator a foot away. I extended my arms and pointed my hands at the indicator, and when I moved my hands, the indicator followed them across the board, onto the table, and off the table to the floor. Lisa and her friends were dumb with amazement.

I decided to tell them about all my strange experiences. Perhaps because Lisa and her friends were young and open-minded, I felt that though they might not understand all I told them (neither did I!) they'd take my story seriously. Lisa was understanding, but she gave my secret away the next day, telling our older sister, Roberta, what she'd seen and the stories I'd recounted. When Roberta cornered me to ask if what Lisa had said was true, I knew it was time to tell her everything.

Pandemonium exploded in the family. My parents demanded to hear the whole story, and for the third time I tried to explain the craziness that had taken hold of my life during the past year and a half. Mom and Dad took it quite well, even when they saw me psychokinetically move a hard candy out of a bowl on the living room table. They were dumbfounded that a person could really do such a thing, to say nothing of the fact that their son was the person doing it, but a lot of things were clicking into place for them: This was why I spent so much time with Buddy and Sam, why it sometimes took us three hours to get home from work, why I seemed to be shrouding so much of my life in secrecy. My mother said, as she has repeated so many times since, "I always knew there was something strange in his eyes." When my parents saw spasms shake my body and a look of pain cross my face as I collapsed from the exertion of performing PK, the harm I might be doing to my health was their greatest concern. For me, it was an enormous relief to share my secret with them at last.

•   •   •

My first conscious expedition into healing took place on Sunday, January 24, 1974, in our tiny apartment. I had decided to show off my abilities, and I confess that it was an ego trip—I wanted to see the amazement on people's faces when they saw me move an object without touching it. My parents, Lisa, Roberta and her husband, Harvey, and their daughter, and assorted aunts and uncles were present.

My niece, Maura, then six years old, shyly pointed out an orange fruit-filled candy lying at the bottom of a glass dish full of cellophane-wrapped sweets. Then I pointed my hands toward the dish, some three feet away, and closed my eyes. I pictured a thin ray of light connecting my hands to the candy Maura had selected. I began to see the candy as an extension of my body. There was no room for doubt; my concentration had to be perfect. When I raised my hands the orange ball started wiggling slowly up from the bottom of the dish, displacing the other candies, then shot out of the bowl to a far corner of the room. I collapsed in a heap.

A couple of hours later—everyone was still buzzing about what they had seen—I noticed that my brother-in-law, Harvey, was rubbing his temples and forehead, complaining that one of his migraines had come on. He headed for the bathroom to get some painkillers, but I called him back. "Wait, don't take the pills, Harv. Sit here in this straight-backed chair."

I didn't really understand why I had spoken to him, or what I was about to do. I simply felt compelled to place my left hand about half an inch from the back of Harvey's neck and my right hand just over his forehead, barely touching him. I closed my

eyes, and a funny, familiar feeling came over me—
a feeling of oneness with Harvey and an intense
desire to give of myself, to help him. At first I
couldn't place the sensation, and then I remembered
the woman who'd been hit by the car in front of
Buddy's—when I had stroked her forehead I had experienced the same feeling. I shivered as I made the
connection between the two events.

Continuing to hold my hands close to Harvey's
head, I found myself doing much the same thing I did
during psychokinesis—relaxing, breathing deeply,
and imagining a oneness, but this time between
myself and another person. It seemed almost as
though I were doing psychokinesis to Harvey—as
though something might be out of place inside his
head and I could move it around. I noticed my concentration didn't seem to be quite as intense as when
I did PK, and I felt strong, rather than depleted.

After about two minutes I relaxed and looked at
Harvey. He was smiling and blushing from ear to
ear. He started hitting his forehead with the palm of
his hand in amazement. "The pain is gone!" he said.
As he told Roberta what he felt, she exclaimed that it
was the first time in ten years that Harvey hadn't had
to take a painkiller for his migraine.

I was more stunned than either of them. What had
I done?

3.

Early Healings

After the dramatic improvement in my father's health became apparent in March 1974, word of my "vibrating hands" and their effects on illness and pain circulated quickly. Knowing that I had helped Dad and Harvey, relatives and friends soon began asking, sometimes begging, me to help them with their health problems. I was struck by how willing people were to try almost anything to relieve their various illnesses. When I questioned those who came to me about their doctor's diagnoses and treatments, it seemed that medical science had run out of answers for most of these people, whose ailments included backaches, migraine headaches, arthritis, multiple sclerosis, paralysis, and cancer.

For me it was an education in the limitations of traditional medicine. I had little knowledge of medicine or disease, and I was surprised that so many people with chronic ailments could not be helped by doctors. I felt impelled to create healing sessions for these desperate people. And though I still had no explanation for what was happening, after our sessions together some of the backache sufferers were without pain, a cousin's depression was lifted, and an uncle's arthritic arm grew less stiff.

As I did more and more healing I evolved a basic technique. Before I began I would concentrate on quieting my mind, blanking out all thoughts and tension, and relaxing my body by taking a number of slow deep breaths. My intuition led me to these relaxation techniques, but I have since learned that they are very similiar to meditative exercises used in such disciplines as transcendental meditation and pranayama yoga.

Having relaxed my mind and body, I usually spent five to ten minutes with each sick person, during which it seemed to me that I was giving him or her a "dose" of my energy. I've never been entirely comfortable using the word *energy* in connection with what I do, since no one has ever established that there is a transfer of energy involved, but from the first time I did psychokinesis, it seemed to me that something like energy (in my mind I saw light) was coming out of me and connecting to the object, and a similar model seemed to apply to healing. Indeed, almost all the people I worked with claimed to feel a pulsating energy, like electricity, passing into their bodies, often accompanied by a sensation of warmth. Visualizing the person's problem area was very important. If a person had a cancerous tumor I would visualize the fleshy malignant mass. Then I would place my hands about half an inch above the skin over the affected area, at the same time imagining the diseased tumor beginning to disintegrate and dissolve. The more vividly I could visualize the troubled spot the more satisfied I was with my interaction with the ill person.

As more and more people came to me for treatment, it became difficult to continue working full-time at Buddy's, so I gradually cut my hours to part-time. Soon I realized I would have to choose between my old life and this strange, exciting new power that had turned my life in an entirely unexpected direction. Finally, and not without some qualms, I left Buddy's Music Store to devote my time to healing.

By that time some of the people who came to me for healing had begun to give me financial contributions, and my parents agreed to help me, so with my small savings I thought I would be able to maintain myself. The decision to give up a conventional means of making a living was made easier by the gratification I felt when people reported they felt better after my treatments, even after their doctors had given up on their cases.

I continued to see "clients" in my parents' apartment, and Mom and Dad took the invasion of their home in stride; they tried to help me in any way they could. They bought me a beautiful wooden desk, which was given a prime location in the living room, and a leather recliner for people to lie on, and they even put folding doors between the living room and the den to form a waiting room. Later I would move to more professional quarters, but there was a certain charm to my first "office." Anyone waiting to see me was ushered into the kitchen to be fed cake and coffee and to be pampered by my mother. My younger sister, Lisa, who had to dodge strangers to get to her room, was still a teenager, and my healing sessions were often carried out to the sound of her stereo blaring through the apartment.

• • •

My first real skeptic was Les Draizen. A jewelry manufacturer in his mid-thirties, Les had arthritis in his right knee, and even cortisone injections had failed to relieve his shoulder; his wife had practically dragged him there.

I started working on his knee, and all of a sudden I saw his face start to turn red. Then he started hitting his knee, standing up and sitting down, and exclaiming, "It's gone! It's gone!" Les had come into my office boisterous and angry, but he walked out like a kitten.

One of the most challenging cases of those early days was that of Pauline Sheinis, a sixty-seven-year-old woman who had been partially paralyzed from the neck down and totally paralyzed from the waist down for over five years, due to complications of a severe spinal abnormality that had developed during one of five strokes. From the moment I first saw her sitting in her wheelchair I knew I was going to try my best to help Pauline walk again.

On the advice of my sister Roberta and her husband, Harvey, Pauline's son Marvin, a real estate agent, arranged to pick me up in Brooklyn one cold, wet April afternoon and take me to see his mother in the Bronx. Pauline was suffering from constant racking headaches, which sometimes brought her close to passing out. She didn't believe in psychic healing, but after hearing about the relief I had given Harvey from his migraine, she had agreed to let Marvin bring me to treat her.

When Pauline, in her wheelchair, greeted Marvin and me at the door, I immediately had a strong feeling that I should work on her spine and legs as well as on her headaches. I'd never worked on paralysis before, but this seemed as good a time as any to experiment. Pauline had nothing to lose, for her doctors had told her she'd never walk again. I decided to say nothing to Pauline, however, for fear of giving her false hope. I had learned early on never to make a promise or guarantee to improve someone's health.

We sat for a while at the kitchen table, and Pauline was politely skeptical as she told me that she didn't believe in healing, but had agreed to give it a try at Marvin's insistence. Her headaches had become so painful that it was sometimes difficult for her to think or even to breathe. At one point she had sought help at a special headache clinic, but the medication they had administered hadn't even taken the edge off her pain.

After making notes on Pauline's history I wheeled her into the living room. I stood behind her and closed my eyes and felt myself slipping into a calm healing state. When I touched her shoulders she jumped and asked me if I had a vibrator under my skin. I laughed and showed her that I was using only my hands, then placed them in another position— one on her right temple and the other on the back of her head. This combination of points felt right—I sensed energy flowing smoothly into Pauline's body—and moments later she quietly murmured that her headache was gone. She called to her husband, Harry, that the pain in her head had vanished.

Then I moved my hands, first up and down Pauline's spinal column, then to her hips, her ankles, and to points under her knees and arms. When she asked in surprise if I was working on her paralysis, I explained that it was only an experiment and that she shouldn't expect anything to come of my attempts.

Pauline assured me she was happy just to receive relief from her headaches.

I began visiting Pauline twice a week, and soon I thought of her and Harry almost as grandparents. Whenever I stopped by we'd sit and talk over bagels and coffee. After about a month of treatments Pauline began to experience pain in her legs. I was momentarily concerned, but then we both became ecstatic, because for her to feel any sensation at all in her dead limbs was a welcome miracle. Within another three or four weeks, the pain diminished, but Pauline's overall sensation continued to grow. Soon she could flex her big toe, and then, slowly, she gained control of all her toes, her ankles, her knees. Finally she was able to work herself out of her wheelchair and onto crutches, for the first time in five years. After several months of sessions Pauline was able to move quite well with just a cane, and ultimately—her treatment stretched to about two years—she was able to walk without any support at all.

Pauline's recovery was so gradual that it was a long time before its significance really struck me. And honestly, after the experience with the door locks in Buddy's car, I thought nothing could ever really amaze me again. Pauline's recovery finally hit me one night when a New York television station that had gotten wind of my healing efforts featured me on the evening news. Pauline had been in my office when the reporters came, and at six o'clock and again at eleven o'clock, I watched the tapes of her moving about on her crutches. Suddenly I found myself shaking my head in wonder. "My God," I said to myself. "She got out of that wheelchair!"

Rabbi Herman Gold, as I'll call him, first came to

see me at my folks' apartment about the same time I started treating Pauline. He was in his late forties, short and round, and very jovial despite the fact that he was in great pain. He had bone cancer, and the prognosis was poor, for the cancer was in his ribs and spine. He'd been through chemotherapy and an enormous number of radiation treatments.

I'm not religious, but Rabbi Gold was a warm man, and I opened up about myself to him more than to anyone else at that time. He used to tell me that often when he was in pain, he'd think about me and the pain would go away. He said he would almost smell my after-shave.

Within about six treatments over six weeks, Rabbi Gold's health seemed to be coming back. He returned to work. Then, he suffered a sudden relapse. He called me from the hospital and asked me to come there to treat him. But his relatives—he didn't have immediate family—wouldn't let me in. They were rigid people, and they just didn't believe in psychic healing.

I was a bit naive about attitudes toward healing then. Today I know that probably ninety percent of the people who come to see me will want to hide it from some member of their family—a husband from his wife, a wife from her husband, a parent from his or her kids.

Shortly after I was rebuffed by Rabbi Gold's family I heard through another client that he had died. What a terrible loss I felt that day. And what a hurt, for he had called for me. I couldn't help but think that if I had been able to treat him just one more time, it might have helped. Rabbi Gold was the first person I ever treated who died.

During the early months of my healing practice I

had been thrust into the center of an emotional tornado. The effect of my successes on me was overpowering. It was enormously satisfying to me to be able to bring smiles and sometimes tears of joy to the faces of people who had given up hope of a pain-free existence. I found myself respected and admired, and I loved every moment of the attention. But there were times of intense self-doubt, and my failure with Rabbi Gold was devastating.

As I plunged deeper and more irrevocably into my new life as a healer it became important for me to find out everything that might be known about healing abilities such as mine. The same questions came back to me again and again. Why did *I* seem to have this special gift? What *really* was happening when I concentrated on releasing "energy"? Why did most of the people I treated feel better immediately or within a short time? And even more important, why didn't they *all* get better?

4.

Yoko and John

My client turned down the lights in his elegant suite, sat down on the floor and drew himself into the cross-legged lotus position. Crouching behind him, I gently placed my hands on his head and neck. I was in my glory! Here I was, treating John Lennon of the Beatles!

Ironically, perhaps, it was my search for answers to my questions about healing that had led me, though indirectly, to this moment. Knowing that I was not entirely at ease in my new role as a healer, my sister Roberta had told me about a social worker-psychologist at Nassau Community Hospital with whom she had spoken about me. He was familiar with psychic phenomena and was eager for me to contact him.

At first I was hesitant, afraid the doctor might think I was some kind of nut, but the desire to learn more about healing and other psychic events led me to call. He listened to my story with a warm and reassuring manner, then recommended that I contact Dr. Karlis Osis, director of New York's American Society for Psychical Research (ASPR), one of the main East Coast bodies devoted to research into parapsychology. He thought Dr. Osis might be able to provide some answers to my questions. Encouraged, I made an appointment.

In a four-story brownstone on the Upper West Side of Manhattan, Dr. Osis and his associate at ASPR, physicist James Merriweather, taped my account of the clicks I had witnessed in Buddy's car and many of my subsequent experiences of clairvoyance and healing. The two men seemed to find my story fascinating, but to my disappointment, Dr. Osis told me at the conclusion that the ASPR was not then equipped to test healing. The society had recently received a legacy of $200,000 earmarked for the purpose of studying the existence of a person's "soul" after physical death, so that had become their focus for the time being. Still, James Merriweather was very interested in my healing work, and the two of us arranged another meeting to plan specific healing experiments that the ASPR might eventually conduct, so I felt somewhat heartened.

I was about to leave the ASPR when the phone rang and a voice yelled for me wait. I returned and found James on the phone with Yoko Ono, the wife of former Beatle John Lennon. James was a friend of Yoko's secretary, Sarah, and by coincidence Yoko was looking for a recommendation for a psychic healer.

James quickly told Yoko about me, explaining that we had just met and that he really knew nothing about me other than what I had told him. To my astonishment, Yoko said she got good feelings about me, so James handed me the phone and Yoko and I made plans to meet at her home the following day.

When I walked out of the ASPR, I felt like I was flying. I must have called up the whole world when I got home. Then I started thinking about healing Yoko. I wanted desperately to help her. All my attitudes at that time had been shaped by the music business, and even though I had rededicated myself to healing, somehow I couldn't help thinking that this could be my "big break."

The next morning I was very nervous. Sam Sunshine and I drove into Manhattan in my old white '63 Buick Riviera, and when we got to Yoko's building, Sam sat outside in the car to wait for me. Yoko lived in the Dakota Apartments, a dark and somber building decorated with eerie gargoyles that was used as a set in the filming of *Rosemary's Baby*. After being announced by the doorman, I rode the elevator to her floor.

Sarah Seagull, Yoko's secretary, let me into the luxurious ten-room apartment. By then I was so awed at the idea of meeting Yoko that I was almost numb, although I really knew nothing about her, other than her connection with John Lennon. Then she appeared, and I was struck first by her stature—she was very, very small—and by her very long hair, which reached well down her thighs.

Yoko invited me into her large kitchen, where we sat in directors' chairs sipping coffee and talking about healing. Yoko spoke in a very relaxed and clear way, and I realized that she was far more learned and sophisticated than I. When the conversation turned to her health, she told me she had been suffering from severe fatigue. We moved into the next room, which was dominated by a dining table and a sculpture consisting of a cube and a pair of jeans, both painted silver. Yoko sat in a straight-backed chair, and I began the laying on of hands.

As I treated Yoko I could see her physical rigidness start to ease, and I felt that she had begun to trust me. Ten minutes passed, and Yoko said that she could feel intense energy moving into her and that she felt strong and full of life. Her smile, a surprise after her early somberness, expressed even more clearly how she felt. Yoko and I sat and chatted for another hour, then set up a schedule of regular appointments covering the next three or four months. As I was leaving, Sarah thanked me, confiding that Yoko hadn't looked so happy in months.

During the first session, I had noticed a small, red rash on Yoko's face. By the time I reached home, a similar rash had broken out on my face in exactly the same location! I was startled, for I'd never considered the possibility of picking up a condition from a client. Then to my amazement, Yoko called that night to report that *her* rash had suddenly disappeared!

After I hung up the phone, I studied my reflection in a mirror. Suddenly I felt a surge of anger, and I yelled aloud to the empty room, "I won't allow it! I won't be in a position to pick up someone else's symptoms!"

The next morning the mysterious rash was gone, but the incident made me realize that I had better protect myself. To me that meant that I must, through concentration keep my "energy charge" so high, so positive, during healings that I would be unable to receive any negativity from the ill person. Since then, no similar incidents have occurred. The ways of healing were a continuous discovery to me.

After my second session with Yoko, she asked what she owed me, and I told her that my policy was to let clients make whatever donation they could afford and felt was appropriate. Those with little money paid nothing at all. When Yoko wrote me a check for a great deal more than I was accustomed to receiving, I expressed some discomfort. Yoko chided me.

"You know," she said, "if you are going to practice healing on a full-time basis, Dean, you have to have money to live on." Yoko had a strong sense of life as a balanced system of exchanges between people.

"An unrewarded service disturbs a relationship," she explained. She smiled, "One must graciously accept fair remuneration for a service, Dean," and she gently pressed the check into my hand. "When each person gives and each person receives, a balance is maintained."

Though I had always felt reasonably comfortable about donations I received from clients, it was reassuring to hear Yoko's reasoning. Throughout my career I've encountered people who think that a healer who accepts money is "unsaintly," that accepting payment somehow taints the healing, and that one can even "lose the gift" by charging for it. I think this is nonsense. I don't believe in exploiting suffering people, but I do think an exchange of fair compensation for the benefits of healing is a reasonable idea.

For a period of months I was at Yoko's house almost every day. From the day I met her I dreamed of meeting her husband, one of the great innovators in popular music. She and John were living separately at the time, but they stayed in touch with one another—indeed, in Yoko's words, John was "courting" her again. At last Yoko invited me to join John and her at the apartment one evening. I was excited when John arrived, doubly excited when he arrived with singer Harry Nilsson. John was slighter than I'd expected, and his hair was reddish, rather than dark. There I was, sitting in Yoko's living room with Yoko, John Lennon, and Harry Nilsson, pinching myself and trying to believe it was all real.

Yoko had warned me before John arrived that "John doesn't think you really help me physically; he thinks it's psychological help." That made me defensive before I met him. At the time I was extremely vulnerable to any criticism, direct or indirect. I myself was uncertain about whether I helped people physically or psychologically, and I adhered to the sharp distinction between mind and body that marks Western thought. But I clung to the idea that it didn't matter *how* I helped my clients, as long as they felt and showed improvement in their health.

Nonetheless, challenged by Lennon's skepticism, I felt compelled to defend myself, and nursing my bruised ego, I decided to counter Lennon's attitude with a demonstration of psychokinesis. If I could just "show him some of my stuff," he would take me more seriously.

Just like my mom, Yoko kept a dish filled to the brim with brightly wrapped, fruit-filled candies, and I asked everyone to be quiet while I sat near it and concentrated deeply, blanking out the people around me and focusing intently on a red candy. I felt as if a beam of light extended from my hands to the candy, and I "grasped" the sweet in my mind. When I moved my hands, I was confident the candy would move. And slowly, it began to wiggle up from the bottom of the dish. We could all hear the cellophane rustling softly as the candy thrust its way up to the top of the pile. My skeptical audience was stunned. Then I focused on four separate candies, mentally gathering them into my "energy field." Psychokinetically I moved them toward me till each dropped over the side of the dish and onto the wooden table. Now the people with me were gasping. I reveled in the control I knew I could exercise. The candies moved toward my outstretched fingers, then scattered in different directions to every corner of the room. I was exhausted and for a moment passed out —the effect PK usually has on me—but when I recovered I felt that I had proven myself.

The effect on the others was dramatic. At first there was dead silence. Then they began bombarding me with questions. John methodically attempted to repeat my demonstration himself, trying as hard as he could to move the candy by staring at it and moving his hands all around it, but he had no luck.

When Lennon put his arm around my shoulder and suggested that we all have dinner at one of John and Yoko's favorite Japanese restaurants, I felt vindicated. And nearly overwhelmed. Walking down the street with John, Yoko, and Harry, I hardly felt my feet touch the street.

The next time I saw John was at the Pierre Hotel in New York, where he and Nilsson were staying; John was producing Nilsson's new album. John had now concluded that the obvious improvement in Yoko's health and attitude was a result of my treatments, so he had decided to book regular sessions for himself.

Lennon wanted what I call a general relaxation treatment, since Yoko had repeatedly extolled the tranquility and sense of well-being that she felt after our sessions together. After I treated him John described feelings of lightheadedness, euphoria, and great relaxation. His attitude had come full circle since our first meeting, and now he seemed to regard me with respect.

When I visited him again at the Pierre, John was having a problem with his electric guitar. Jokingly, he asked, "Do you heal guitars, too, Dean?" I asked for a screwdriver, opened up his guitar, took the guts out, fixed the minor short that was causing the trouble, and put the parts back together again. It played perfectly, and when he had recovered from his amazement, John couldn't stop laughing. My old days at Buddy's had really come in handy!

One afternoon a couple of weeks later, I got a frantic call from John, who was at a midtown recording studio where Harry Nilsson was taping some tracks for his *Pussycat* album. Harry was having vocal problems during the recording of "Save the Last Dance for Me." "Dean, I need you!" John cried. "Harry's losing his voice!" Harry had strep throat, and Lennon hoped a "zap of energy" might help him finish the session. Within half an hour, a block-long limousine pulled up at my building in Sheepshead Bay to take me to Manhattan. I remember how important I felt stepping into that limousine. Most of the people in our neighborhood had probably never even seen a limo of that size—certainly I never had—and I wondered what they would think if they knew where it was taking me. My ego was anything but starved.

When I arrived at the studio people were running around madly and the musicians sat waiting impatiently with their instruments on their laps. Confidently I strode over to Harry. There was no place to sit, and since Harry is six feet four and I'm five feet five, I had to stand on my toes to reach his neck. I put my hands around his throat and began to concentrate. I never work on strep throats and similar infections, because they respond to medication, but I figured that if the muscles in Harry's throat were less tense, it would help his voice.

For a minute the people in the control booth went crazy, thinking that Harry was being choked by some wild man off the streets! The story circulated for months afterward. But the treatment did help ease Harry's taut vocal chords, and he was able to continue with the recording session.

John and Yoko were so enthusiastic about my abilities that they decided they should be made public. Yoko started the ball rolling by arranging my first radio appearance, on a talk show on New York's WOR-AM.

I was very nervous about talking before an unseen audience of hundreds of thousands. Yoko had warned me that long-time radio host Barry Farber was generally unsympathetic to the field of psychic healing, but she said she thought his show would be a good forum for me. During the broadcast Farber seemed to take a liking to me, and he expressed respect for my stand that psychic healing was an ad-

junct to medical science. I made it clear that I wasn't
trying to buck the medical profession, but to supplement it with a last-resort therapy when conventional
methods failed. The phone lines were jammed with
incoming calls, and the studio was buzzing.

My contact with John and Yoko came to an end after
they had reunited and Yoko had given birth to their
son, Sean. At that time, they cut themselves off from
many people with whom they'd been associated,
placing an open letter to their friends in *The New
York Times* explaining their need to share their
privacy with their child.

Then, after five years of seclusion, John and Yoko
had just recorded a new album and begun to resume
a degree of public life when John was slain by a gun-
man outside his home. I had been looking forward to
a renewed friendship, and a terrible emptiness overwhelmed me after John's tragic and nightmarish
murder.

To have Yoko Ono as one of the first healing clients
who came to me from outside the close circle of
family connections and word-of-mouth recommendations was an incredibly heady experience.
Having been a musician and then finding myself involved with Yoko and John was like having a
thousand-watt light shining on me. For a while, I'm
afraid, I developed a tremendous ego.

With time I dropped a lot of that ego, though, and
as I did I felt my healing getting better. Early in my
healing career I felt that I had to constantly prove
myself to people, and I thought that the support of
celebrities meant a lot. It took age and experience for

me to outgrow those attitudes. I'd hate to have missed the times I spent with John and Yoko, for I grew to love them as individuals, but in time celebrity lost a lot of its significance for me. I came to realize that I don't have to continually prove myself or my healing abilities to others. As I've grown more secure within myself, my need for external approval and support has fallen away.

5.

The World of Parapsychology

When one begins to study a new field one quickly discovers the existence of an "inner circle" in that specialty. One encounters, again and again, the same few names—the people who are most acclaimed, most active, most influential or otherwise notable for their accomplishments in the field. If my search for some logical explanation of what happened when I "healed" led indirectly to my first encounters with celebrities and publicity, it also led me, more appropriately, into another special world, one less known by the general public. As I searched for an explanation for all the strange things that were happening to me, I began to meet some of the people most prominently connected with research into paranormal events.

James Merriweather, the physicist who had shown early interest in my work, met with me several times to discuss the possibility of getting the American Society for Psychical Research interested in healing research. In May 1974, he invited me to an ASPR symposium in New York, which he thought would be good opportunity for me to meet some of the other people connected with the society.

Many important people in parapsychology were to lecture at the symposium. Among them were Russell Targ, a physicist from the Stanford Research Institute in California, and Professor Bernard Grad, from McGill University in Canada, who is best known for a variety of healing experiments conducted with Colonel Oskar Estebany, a Russian healer. Professor Gertrude Schmeidler of City College of the City University of New York, who conducted experiments in psychokinesis with psychic Ingo Swann, and Montague Ullman of the "dream lab" at Maimonides Hospital in Brooklyn and a former president of the ASPR, also spoke.

This was my first exposure to the world of psychic research. All day long, in the large auditorium, reports on experiments were presented by one scientist after another. Occasionally there was a witty speaker, but to be honest, the program seemed terribly tedious. But James kept me busy outside meeting people, so I found the experience exciting. An intellectual atmosphere prevailed at the symposium, and for the most part the people in attendance seemed pretty level-headed. I felt very comfortable among them.

Among the people to whom James introduced me was Helen Kruger, a reporter for *The Village Voice*. Helen had written one of the first articles about Israeli psychic Uri Geller and was completing a book called *Other Healers, Other Cures*.

Several days after the symposium Helen called to ask if I could come to her apartment to treat a friend who had fallen by her swimming pool. The woman's doctor had told her that she had strained her back and that it would just take time for the pain to subside. I went to Helen's apartment and treated her, however, and her pain disappeared.

After her friend left, Helen began asking me about the experiences that had led me to healing. I was growing so uneasy about discussing my experience with the clicking door locks—obviously people didn't believe it—that I gave her Buddy's and Sam's phone numbers so she could call them for confirmation of what I was telling her.

Then, abruptly, Helen walked over to a bookshelf and returned with a set of keys. She asked me if I'd ever tried to do psychometry. When I said I'd never *heard* of psychometry, she explained that it was the ability to discern emotion or information from an inanimate object.

I took the keys, sat back in my chair, closed my eyes and emptied my mind of outside thoughts. I began rubbing the keys with my fingers, and like a flash I saw an image of a middle-aged woman! Suddenly my hand and then my entire arm began to shake. My head began to pound. It was a struggle to speak.

"Something's wrong," I gasped. "I don't feel well. . . . This woman's dead!"

"How old?" Helen asked excitedly.

"About forty-five," I told her. "I feel something tragic, some severe emotional distress."

I didn't like the way I felt, and, afraid to hold the keys any longer, I dropped them to the floor. The pounding inside my head and the shaking of my arm began to subside. Helen had been watching me intensely, hanging on every word I said, and she was obviously taken aback. The keys had belonged to a forty-five-year-old friend of hers, she told me. The friend had just died of a heart attack, which seemed to have been brought on by a series of deep personal crises!

I was excited that I had been able to perceive these pieces of information, but I didn't care for the physical and emotional discomforts that seemed to accompany psychometry. The experience was unnerving, and I wasn't eager to try it again.

"I've got to call Judy; I've got to call Judy," Helen exclaimed, and she immediately phoned Judy Skutch, whose Foundation for Parasensory Investigation conducted extensive research into parapsychology. Everything was happening so fast. I had seen Judy Skutch at the symposium, trailed by a large group of obviously dedicated followers. Now Helen was arranging for me to meet her, one of the most powerful backers and sympathizers in the field of parapsychology.

That very night we went to see Judy, who lived with her stockbroker husband in a grand apartment building on Manhattan's Upper West Side. The elevator delivered us to two gold-trimmed doors, the private entrance to Judy's elegant multiroomed apartment. A number of other people were also there to see her.

When my turn came, Judy—attractive, slim, freckle-faced and very young looking—listened closely to my account of my adventures. She had already heard from Helen about my healing of her friend and my psychometry experience, and at Judy's request I worked on several people on the spot and helped them with various ailments.

Judy was warm, sympathetic, vivacious, and ambitious, and I liked her at once. I was thrilled when she promised that her foundation would help support my healing efforts and that she would involve me in some research the foundation sponsored. She suggested we put together a proposal for the work we felt was most important, and we quickly agreed that our first goal should be an attempt to see whether I controlled an energy that could be measured scientifically. Judy said she wanted to introduce me to many people in the parapsychology field, and she wanted to meet my parents.

A week later, flanked by Mom and Dad, my sisters, and my brother-in-law, I went nervously to Judy's home. Among her other guests were Ingo Swann, who had conducted many experiments with "out-of-body" experiences, and Brendan O'Regan, a scientist who had worked with Buckminster Fuller and now serves as director of the Institute of Noetic Sciences in Palo Alto, California. Everyone listened to my healing cases with such interest that the anxiety with which I had approached the gathering seemed unwarranted. I found myself enjoying the stimulating conversation of scientists, psychics, and doctors. I felt at home and welcome, and so did my family. I was a bit in awe of Judy, and very grateful that she wanted me under her wing.

As Judy and I came to know each other she told me how she had become so deeply involved in psychic work. For some time, she had been fascinated with the inexplicable incidents of apparent clairvoyance and telepathy that she, like so many people, encountered in daily life. She always wondered about odd coincidences—how did it happen that the name of a person she hadn't seen in years would come to mind, only to be followed by a call, a letter, or news of that very person? Most people are too busy or too skeptical to pay attention to such occurrences, but Judy was very sensitive, and several seemingly psychic experiences with her young daughter had led her to become involved with the American Society for Psychical Research.

For ten years Judy had been supporting and campaigning for research into paranormal phenomena through her Foundation for Parasensory Investigation. In 1973 she had been one of the founding members of the Institute of Noetic Sciences; another founder was Apollo 14 astronaut Edgar D. Mitchell. The institute's primary interest at its founding was the scientific investigation of psychic phenomena, and the organization had collaborated with Judy's foundation in several psi—short for psychic—experiments. Judy had also worked for the establishment of accredited college courses in the study of parapsychology, and in the early seventies New York University established a full-credit course, which she taught.

Judy had been one of the first people in the country to whom Uri Geller was introduced. Dr. Andrija Puharich, a physician involved in parapsychology, had met Geller in Israel and had become fascinated with this lanky, goodlooking young man's unusual metal-bending and telepathic abilities. Dr. Puharich had contacted Judy, Edgar Mitchell, as well as two laser physicists at the Stanford Research Institute, Russell Targ and Dr. Harold Puthoff, and had finally convinced them of the validity of Geller's powers. Judy had been impressed enough to seek financial backing for scientific studies of Geller's activities.

Eventually Geller's work generated a lot of controversy. Various publications expressed skepticism, not only about Geller, but about his supporters and all the institutions that were involved in research with him.

At about the same time, a researcher working at Duke University had been conducting experiments that he claimed demonstrated extrasensory perception in rats. The parapsychologist had presented his findings at many psi conferences, where, for the most part, they had been enthusiastically accepted. When *The New York Times* revealed that the researcher had tampered with his results in order to produce the desired effect, his unethical behavior cast a shadow over the entire field. Thus, it was a gloomy time for research into psychic phenomena. As a newcomer, I was unaware of this situation.

Therefore the timing of my meeting with Judy was fortuitous for me. Judy had a genuine interest in helping mankind through healing, and she was eager to find a new vehicle for her powerful energies. I found her interest and attention encouraging and helpful, and I was more than happy to find a qualified guide through the maze of scientific bureaucracy.

Judy talked constantly about the importance of doing research to verify my special powers. I agreed with her priorities, for a medical-scientific explanation of what I was doing was still important to me. Knowledge of the positive effects people received from my treatments had persuaded me to set aside my constant self-questioning and follow my intuition, but I still wanted and needed scientific authentication of what I did.

As Judy introduced me to various figures in parapsychology, I learned more about how my abilities were perceived. Most researchers were stunned that I could apparently turn my "energy" on and off at will. I was told that psychics usually don't have such control, and some can only perform in a favorable and supportive environment.

I discussed the moving door locks in Buddy's car with several parapsychologists, and it was suggested to me more than once that my subconscious might have been at work, psychokinetically moving the locks and thus originating the messages, the whole time. It requires such intense concentration for me to perform PK that it was difficult for me to imagine doing it subconsciously, but I wanted to find a reasonable explanation for those messages, and I found this theory intriguing, if not altogether satisfying.

From the very beginning, Judy's beliefs in my "powers" was evidently very strong, and after I introduced her to Pauline Sheinis, the woman who had spent five years in a wheelchair, Judy was even more impressed. But it was an unscheduled demonstration of psychokinesis that finally unleashed the full strength of Judy's enthusiasm on my behalf.

Pauline had left, and I was sitting with Judy in her living room. My insides were jumping with nervous excitement, for all afternoon I'd felt the urge to demonstrate PK for Judy. I borrowed the pen she was making notes with and decided to make it trail my hands across the rug. I lay the pen about two feet away, and as I concentrated on forming the necessary mental connection, it began to move. In a flash Judy was on the floor beside me, an experienced observer obviously checking for trickery.

As usual I passed out momentarily from the exertion, and I awoke to find Judy holding my wrist and checking my pulse. When I asked her what my pulse rate was, she said I wouldn't want to know, but I could tell my heart was racing.

Within minutes Judy was on the phone, calling associates in California, planning a research trip for me and clearly reveling in the idea of presenting her new protégé. I listened with admiration as the next chapter in my new "career" was plotted for me. I might have felt like a puppet, except that puppets have no say in how they move. Judy and I shared the same hopes and aims for my work—we were both eager to establish some kind of scientific verification of my strange "powers." I saw myself moving into the scientific arena in the company of a formidable ally.

6.

Getting Established

The next step in Judy's plans was a guest lecture at her parapsychology class at New York University, an interview with a *Village Voice* reporter, and a number of appearances on local radio. The day after one of my radio interviews aired, a piece of the past slammed back into my life with the return of a woman whose importance to me was to be even greater than Judy's. I answered the phone and immediately recognized the voice of Rochelle Gromadzin, a young woman I had dated steadily several years before.

I had met Rochelle when I was eighteen, one Saturday afternoon when I was working at Buddy's. She was dark, slim, and attractive, an accomplished classical accordianist, and though she was only fifteen she looked a lot older. We had begun to spend a great deal of time together.

We had even made plans to marry when Rochelle graduated from high school, but shortly before the incidents with the clicks in Buddy's car began, Rochelle and I had started to fight frequently and pointlessly. Perhaps we both knew we were really too young to settle down. Still, our final breakup had left me feeling numb and empty. After that, we had gradually lost touch. The last time I had spoken to Rochelle, she had called to tell me of her impending marriage. It had been a painful conversation.

Now Rochelle was on the phone telling me that she had left her husband. I teased her a bit about acting impetuously, for I'd been dating another girl for some time and I didn't think Rochelle's life was of too much concern to me anymore.

Abruptly Rochelle changed the subject and started asking what "crazy nonsense" I was now involved in—she had heard me talking about healing and psychokinesis on the radio the night before. There was no mistaking the genuine, concerned interest in her voice. She suggested we get together that same evening, but I had promised Judy I would complete the long overdue story of my healing career, and I still had to type it all. Rochelle immediately offered to type it for me. She was a crackerjack typist, so the work would soon be out of the way, leaving the rest of the evening free for us to get reacquainted.

I went to pick Rochelle up at her parent's house, where she was now living. When she came to the door and I saw her once again, with her lustrous dark hair and her huge sad brown eyes, I felt all my old feelings for her come flooding back.

That evening we brought each other up to date on our adventures and growth in the last few years. Rochelle seemed to accept the changes in my life easily. I gave her a sample of a healing treatment, and she gasped with amazement when she felt electrical vibrations in her legs while I was touching her temples.

I went back to her parents' house for dinner the next night, and Rochelle persuaded her skeptical father to let me treat his chronic tennis elbow. His pain went away. That made me feel so good, so rambunctious that in the middle of dinner I grabbed a can of soda, pulled off the metal tab, and instructed everyone to follow me into the living room. Dropping down onto the green shag carpet, I placed the tab about three feet in front of me. I closed my eyes, concentrated and felt the energy rising within me, then pointed my hands at the shiny tab and began pulling them back toward my body. As I knew it would, the tab followed—slowly at first, then jerking its way across the thick rug.

"My God! It's really moving!" Rochelle's dad blurted.

"Ssshhh!" Rochelle hushed him. She never took her eyes off the tab or my hands. At first she seemed a bit frightened by what she was seeing, but within a few moments her fear gave way to excitement over the display of this new ability.

From the first night we saw each other again, Rochelle and I realized that we belonged together. We resumed our old relationship, and within days Rochelle left her job to help me in my work, doing the organizational and secretarial tasks and serving as my receptionist. A few months later we became engaged, and in December 1975, we married.

In Rochelle I have found a true partner in life. Her desire to help me and be my companion in work and play has always made my strange life seem more sane and normal. With her loving, positive attitude, she has grounded my high-intensity, live-wire personality, calmed me, and helped relieve some of the tensions generated by my healing career. We have become a team, constantly trying to supplement and support each other when the pressures of our life become rough.

The first time I was to meet Judy after Rochelle and I had reunited, I took Rochelle along. I was bursting with happiness about our restored relationship, and I wanted to proclaim it to the world. I certainly wanted these two very important women in my life to know each other. And indeed, they seemed to have immediate rapport.

Judy had a big surprise of her own for me. She announced excitedly that the arrangements for my first research trip were complete. On November 7—only three months away—I was going to California for a week of tests.

The phone rang and Judy ran to get it, and Rochelle and I talked quietly in the kitchen.

"I wish I could come with you to California," Rochelle said wistfully, knowing full well that neither of us had enough money to pay for her airfare.

We were sunk in mutual disappointment when Judy tore back into the kitchen, looking like the cat who had swallowed the canary.

"Kid," she said, looking right at Rochelle, "how would you like to go to San Francisco with Dean?"

"I'd love to!" Rochelle cried, throwing her arms around Judy.

Judy was banking that my test results in California would be better if I were as comfortable and relaxed as possible. If that meant Rochelle accompanying me, Rochelle would accompany me. I was overjoyed.

In the weeks that followed, Judy thrust me into a dizzy whirl of meetings aimed at creating interest in my work and opening old-fashioned minds. We needed to raise funds for our upcoming research, so there were meetings with prominent and wealthy parapsychology sympathizers. Judy felt free to call me at any time of day or night to arrange meetings with potential supporters. I enjoyed the challenge of trying to open people's minds to healing, even though the pace was sometimes tiring. With Judy's verbal persuasiveness and my persuasive touch, we were a winning team.

Among the many people to whom Judy introduced me was a pilot, whom I'll call Jack Shays, who suffered from angina pectoris. Doctors had told him that the blood vessels around his heart were partially closed, prohibiting the free flow of blood. Jack could suffer a heart attack at any time, and consequently his pilot's license had been revoked. I wanted to help, and I was eager to try working on such a heart condition, so I offered to treat him.

For the first session I traveled to upstate New York, where Jack, tall and silver-haired at fifty-five, welcomed me to his suburban home. He was enthusiastic and eager to begin treatment. Over the next month I treated him four more times in my Brooklyn office. After each treatment Jack would go to New York Hospital to have an electrocardiogram taken, hoping that the machine would reveal a lessening of his arterial blockage. Each time the reading came back unchanged. After the fifth test, I told Jack I didn't think I could help him.

He brushed my remark aside. "Hey, I'm not looking for a miracle," he said. "Why don't we try a few more sessions? Maybe some people need more treatments than others. I'm willing to keep trying if you are. I have nothing to lose."

Of course he was right. Why should I limit myself by expecting results after only five sessions? Most people were helped by fewer treatments, but that didn't mean everyone needed the same number of sessions.

After Jack's seventh visit, he got, after all, a miracle. His EKG was suddenly normal. His license was restored after the unexplained and unanticipated healing of his angina—a condition that usually grows steadily worse—and soon Jack was flying again.

His thanks were heartfelt, but not nearly as gratifying as the lesson he had taught me: Never put limits on yourself. After knowing Jack, I felt that I could learn from every person with whom I came in contact.

The patience and persistence that Jack taught me were valuable when I treated lively Irma Bacharach, mother of composer Burt Bacharach. Irma came to me suffering with osteoporosis, a demineralizing or loss of calcium from bones. This degenerative disease, which most commonly affects petite women over fifty, can eventually make bones so brittle that they break from a simple bruise. Irma, in her seventies, had such pain in her hips, knees, ankles, and spine that she could walk only a little, and then only very slowly with the aid of two canes. In fact, she bought a mirror for us to hang near the door of the office, for she was very conscious of her appearance and liked to fix her hair after she arrived, but couldn't manage the fifteen-foot walk from the waiting room to the bathroom. Irma's legs and ankles were so swollen that she was uncomfortable wearing skirts.

After several treatments there was only slight improvement in Irma's condition. Then, suddenly, after thirteen weeks, Irma got well. With great joy she phoned to tell me that she had walked fifteen blocks! Then she began to forget her canes. Soon she was completely free of pain, and her doctor announced that she had gone into "remission."

Judy always stressed the importance of the medical profession's acceptance of psychic healing, and because of her influence I became more and more interested in medicine and the medical uses of my healing ability. Several doctors to whom Judy introduced me eventually became personal friends, and they gave me medical references, such as *The Merck Manual* and Harrison's *Principles of Internal Medicine,* that enabled me to communicate with doctors using their own terminology.

Clients who were helped by my treatments widened my circle of medical contacts by telling their doctors about me. I was eager to share my ideas with any doctors who would talk with me, always with the aim of setting up research at their respective hospitals, for the question of what I was actually doing to the human body never left my mind.

Whenever I encountered new patients I made it a point to find out if they had exhausted all conventional medical channels before coming to me. Then I requested recent diagnoses of their illnesses from their doctors. Before I treated a new case I studied the symptoms, causes, and procedures usually employed to ease the problem. I found that the more information I had about a person's condition the better I was able to visualize the ailment. Some psychics and healers practice "psychic diagnosing," but I would always want medical confirmation of such a diagnosis. I believe that the mind can create illness and that the mind can cure, and some people are so suggestible that if a psychic told them they had a certain illness their minds might produce the condition.

Before long doctors began calling me in on problem cases. One such physician, Dr. Abraham Weinberg, heard of me from Judy and requested my help with a tough case of herpes zoster, or shingles. For two months, the patient had been suffering excruciating pain from swollen sores on her torso.

As I concentrated on radiating energy over the patient's afflicted area I visualized a stimulated blood flow in the woman's body to help speed the healing. After our first session my energy still felt extremely high, so I impulsively took Dr. Weinberg's fountain pen from his jacket pocket and psychokinetically moved it across his office floor, leaving doctor and patient speechless. Dr. Weinberg called the next day to tell me that the woman's pain was virtually gone and her sores were already less inflamed. I treated her three more times, and within two weeks the shingles were gone. Dr. Weinberg said there was no medical explanation for such rapid improvement.

Some of my patients were themselves intimately involved with the world of traditional medicine. Kyp Susser and her husband, Dr. Murray Susser, who is a member of the board of directors of the International Academy of Preventive Medicine and on the teaching staff of St. Margaret's Hospital in Pittsburgh, came to see me about a painful knee ailment that had tortured Kyp for five years. Dr. Susser and other physicians who examined Kyp's knee had been unable to find the cause of her agonizing pain and restricted movement.

When I began to work on Kyp I allowed her husband to hold her hand, for she was quite nervous. I laid my hands successively on her forehead, her shoulders, and her bad knee. Kyp gasped when I touched her. "It feels like an electric shock is going through me!" she said. Even Murray said he felt vibrations passing from her hand to his. That night Kyp Susser recovered full pain-free movement of her knee. I've never had to treat her again. Today she's fully active and even plays tennis.

Another patient was Dr. Howard White, a thirty-nine-year-old clinical psychologist who had worked at the Kingsbridge Veterans Administration Hospital in the Bronx for seventeen years. Howard had suffered a complex of excrutiating symptoms—back and leg pains, loss of bladder control, spasticity in his legs, vertigo, and other neurological problems—for several years, during which he had run the medical gamut trying to have his ailment diagnosed. To his frustration and dismay, most doctors had told him his problem was all in his mind.

It was only after he had fallen heavily on his back and suffered immediate partial paralysis that his doctors realized that his illness wasn't psychosomatic. In fact, he had severe spinal cord compression; a protruding thoracic disc was pressing against the spinal cord, creating the paralysis and other symptoms. Emergency surgery, in which a couple of degenerated discs were removed, alleviated the pressure on his spine. But Howard was left with a great deal of spasticity, muscle atrophy in his legs, back pain, and a deep depression. He learned of my work from a friend and came to see me.

Each time I treated Howard I directed the healing energy into the area of his back where he experienced the greatest pain. I visualized a knotted muscle, sent the energy radiating into it, then "saw" the muscle become looser, more fluid in substance. Howard responded quickly to our sessions. Within weeks his balance improved, the muscle spasms decreased, and his muscle tone began to return. By his own subjective assessment his pain had diminished by eighty percent.

For the first time since the onset of his health problems, Howard, who had once danced professionally with the American Ballet Theater, was able to take ballet classes again. He invited Rochelle and me to attend a class. As I watched him move across the floor with balance and style, I realized that things had been happening so fast that it was often difficult for me to appreciate the changes I was actually creating in people's lives. Experiencing the joy of Howard's recovery made me feel that what I was doing was useful and very much needed. I was very lucky to have been given this gift. The end result—health—was all that really mattered.

Still, my mind drifted back to the same basic, troubling questions. What was the "energy" with which I healed? How did I help people? Was it just psychological—suggestion—or was I affecting the body in a physiological manner? I began putting a lot of thought into my upcoming research trip to California, which I hoped would finally provide me with some answers.

7.

Scientists Put Me to the Test

"There she is!" I shouted, triumphant at finding Judy in the crowded, noisy heart of the San Francisco airport. She stood with a friend to one side of the onrushing crowd, craning her neck to find Rochelle and me.

It was November 7, 1974. I was happy to be in San Francisco, and as eager as Judy to begin the various tests. Judy efficiently steered us through the masses of people to the baggage claim area, and chattered busily as Rochelle and I dragged our tightly packed luggage from the moving belt.

"Five suitcases? Are you staying a week or six months?" she teased.

After spending half an hour working the luggage and ourselves into Judy's tiny rented Pinto I understood her concern. Then, with her friend giving directions and pointing out places of interest, Judy drove through the beautiful hills and curving side streets. In the back seat, Rochelle and I were lost in our own thoughts.

I felt excited and happy, but the trip to California didn't seem quite real to me yet. My whole life as a healer still seemed unreal to me at times. I tried to imagine what Rochelle was feeling—this was all new to her, too. I looked over at her. We were both desperately uncomfortable, bent like pretzels, sitting on top of our luggage, weary from our five-hour flight and hot and sticky in our heavy sweaters.

Soon we drove up in front of a sleek, modern hotel, the Burlingame Hyatt House. Judy disappeared into the lobby, and we got out to stretch our legs. Then Judy emerged with a tall, slim, dapper yet casually dressed man who welcomed us warmly, introducing himself as Bob Williamson, the general manager. He led us up to our suite, where we just had time to drop off our luggage before joining Judy at a smorgasbord luncheon at the Stanford Research Institute (SRI). Russell Targ and Dr. Harold Puthoff, the physicists I'd met at the parapsychology symposium; parapsychologist Brendan O'Regan of the Institute of Noetic Sciences; and Dr. Ted Bastin, a quantum physicist at Cambridge University and part-time research consultant for SRI and Noetics, joined us.

Founded in 1946, Stanford Research Institute is a problem-solving organization—a "think tank"—situated on a seventy-acre expanse in Menlo Park, California, just south of San Francisco and within a few miles of Stanford University, with which it was once affiliated. SRI has branch offices and labs in Europe and the Far East, and often works with federal, state, and city governments in the areas of health, education, and public welfare.

After lunch we toured the parapsychology labs, which consisted of two closet-sized rooms. I was somewhat surprised, for I didn't yet understand the problems faced by scientists seriously interested in exploring paranormal phenomena. Most of the research directors at SRI looked down on parapsychology research. Only a few brave individuals took on work in this delicate and controversial field, and they tried to work quietly, without drawing public attention to their activities. Puthoff and Targ faced a constant battle to acquire even the most meager facilities. Funds for psychic research at SRI came primarily from private individuals, corporations, and psi groups, while most other projects were government-funded and received much more money.

That night Rochelle and I had dinner with Bob Williamson in his apartment at the hotel. As a result of Bob's deep interest in the psychic field, Uri Geller, Ingo Swann, and other psychic research subjects had stayed at the hotel in recent years. Bob enjoyed the company of such people and was eager to develop keener paranormal senses himself.

After dinner we were joined by Dr. Ted Bastin, Brendan O'Regan, and Judy. With candles lending a soothing light to the room and country-and-western music playing softly on the stereo, I felt very relaxed and comfortable with these people, and linked to them by our shared interest in parapsychology. We discussed my upcoming projects at length.

When Dr. Bastin, who had a stretched ligament in his left shoulder, asked if I worked on sore joints, I was delighted to treat him. I felt my energy flowing unusually strongly, and I was not surprised when Dr. Bastin said his pain was decreasing. Then, going deeper into the treatment, I felt a sudden and tremendous rush of energy—the beginning of the urge to do psychokinesis. For a split second, though, I wondered if I would be able to demonstrate my PK ability during this trip. Lately, PK had seemed to be harder and harder on my body—it drained me more than it originally had, and I took longer to recover. Many times I'd wondered if it was wise to continue doing psychokinesis, and whether I might be incurring permanent damage to my body. But shaking off my doubt, I pulled a ballpoint pen from Bob's pocket, knelt on the floor and set it in front of me.

Rochelle and Judy knew at once what I was going to do, and they cleared space in the center of Bob's living room. Everyone gathered around on hands and knees. Staring silently, I saw myself connected to the pen. Then I started to lean back, and the pen started moving toward me. The others were running their hands across the rug, checking for trickery, and they were just astonished by what I was doing. I backed up as far as I could, and then, as usual, I collapsed in exhaustion. But I knew that, regardless of the outcome of the scheduled lab tests, I had demonstrated psychokinesis before a group of trained observers. A weight fell from my shoulders and I began to look forward to the upcoming experiments with real enthusiasm.

Rochelle and I had the next day to ourselves, and we happily explored the windswept city. The next morning, rested and eager to begin work, I was escorted to SRI by Ted Bastin, Brendan O'Regan, Rochelle, Judy, and Dr. Jerry Jampolsky, a child psychiatrist who had published many papers on child behavior in relation to ESP. In the "conference room"—one of the two tiny rooms used for psychic research—we had a brief preliminary meeting. Then Targ and Dr. Puthoff showed me into the next room, where, on a narrow table opposite the door, they had set up a pendulum apparatus covered by a glass bell jar to block out wind and air currents. The room was crowded with equipment—a laser that was focused on a mirror on the pendulum, chart recorders, and what seemed to be an enormous computer.

Our first experiment was intended to see if the pendulum, which was swinging gently in a steady rhythm, might be affected by "healing energy" generated in the room where it stood. Hal Puthoff would act as a patient, and I would "lay hands" on him and try to alter the motion of the pendulum.

I didn't give myself time to think about whether I would be successful. The outcome of the test was important to me, but the fact that I had performed psychokinesis the night before gave me confidence. Hal Puthoff settled himself in a chair with his back to me, and I automatically placed my hands on his shoulders. He had no illness for me to visualize, so I absently began to send energy into Hal's body, holding in my mind a picture of the pendulum apparatus. With my mind's eye I "saw" the pendulum begin to swing in a wider arc under the glass jar.

Immediately Russell Targ, who was watching the chart recorder, yelled, "It's moving! Hal, come here and look at this!"

"Russ, I'm being treated—I can't move!" Hal objected.

I felt a rush of excitement. Deep inside I'd been fairly certain that I'd have an effect on the pendulum, but I'd barely begun the treatment, and even I was surprised when it happened so fast. After a few minutes I withdrew my hands from Hal, and the pendulum returned to its original rhythm.

When Hal looked at the instruments he seemed genuinely surprised. He and Russell had never seen such distinct change in movement before, he told me. When Judy rejoined us, beaming with satisfaction, Hal excitedly told her that the experimental results warranted further testing.

The test marked the first time I had performed PK and healing simultaneously, but I had always felt that they involved the same force. It was my intention and the visualization I created in my mind that determined what the effect would be.

I was exhilarated, but I was also exhausted from all the excitement, as well as from doing PK. As I was leaving the lab Hal told me we would attempt the same experiment the next day. I felt ready and confident.

The next day, Sunday, Bob, Rochelle and I met early for breakfast in the hotel. The results of the previous day's tests had left me feeling exuberant, and I proceeded to order eggs and three portions of hashed brown potatoes, one of my favorite foods. After I wolfed them all down my stomach felt a bit unsettled, but I ignored it. I was eager to get back to SRI.

During the second pendulum experiment Dr. Bastin was the recipient of my energy, and there was great excitement when I repeated the results of the previous day's test. I felt very sure of myself now, and I decided to really show these men what I could do. Leaving one hand "hooked up" to Dr. Bastin, I pointed the other directly toward the pendulum. The pendulum started to make longer, faster swings, tracing a wider and wider arch, until it fell right off its treadle!

Russell and Hal stared at each other and at the charts with amazement and delight. Finally their reserve cracked, and they began yelling and exclaiming, laughing and shaking their heads at what had happened.

I was thrilled to have proved that the first test results weren't a fluke, but I was feeling more and more queasy, and finally I had to excuse myself and take refuge in the men's room to vomit. When I tottered back to the scientists, Rochelle noted my pallor and expressed concern. I felt sheepish, but I knew I wasn't up to continuing that day. I even waited around for a while, hoping to feel better, but as the morning went on I had to accept the fact that my energy gauge read "low."

Hal was very sympathetic and encouraged me to leave. Russell, however, was very annoyed, for he had hoped to accomplish much more that day. I was as disappointed as he, but at least I had successfully repeated the pendulum experiment. Things were looking good, even though, at the moment, I was feeling dreadful!

I woke up on Monday feeling fully restored. Early in the afternoon Judy took Rochelle and me to the Institute of Noetic Sciences in Palo Alto, where we briefly met former astronaut Edgar D. Mitchell, who was pleasant but very reserved. Then we went on to Tiburon, a lovely town across the San Francisco Bay, for a session with Jerry Jampolsky, the psychiatrist. Judy had arranged for Dr. Jampolsky to supervise the monitoring of my brain waves, heart waves, and blood pressure while I treated John Peterson, a reporter for *The National Observer*, the conservative Washington-based newspaper. John had a small, benign tumor on his knee, and he was going to write an article about my efforts to reduce it.

Jerry had a houseboat-office in a unique setting overlooking San Franciso Bay. I was enchanted by the sight of the ferry from San Francisco to Tiburon, which passed his large picture windows every hour.

I chatted with John Peterson while Dr. Jampolsky attached cables for an electrocardiogram (EKG), which monitors heart activity, and an electroencephalogram (EEG), which records brain waves, to each of us. Then Jerry told me to begin the healing. After a few minutes, John fell soundly asleep. This was getting to be one of the two most common reactions to my treatments—either patients were so soothed and tranquilized that they went to sleep, or they got a tremendous rush of energy and could hardly sit still. As John slept in his chair I worked on his knee, concentrating on dissolving the lump of excess tissue.

When I was finished Dr. Jampolsky reported that the EEG readings revealed that during the healing my brain was producing alpha waves, which are associated with relaxation. Many researchers have theorized that psychic happenings occur more frequently when a person is in this tranquil state than when he or she is in a beta, or awake, state.

X rays of John's tumor had been taken before my treatment, and more were taken afterward, but the tumor remained unchanged. However, after John published his article—a good, objective account of our session together—the tumor decreased in size by ninety-five percent, as measured by yet another X ray.

The day after my session with John, Judy, Rochelle, and I traveled to SRI's biomedical division, where I was introduced to Dr. Erik Peper, whose specialty is the different regions of the brain. Dr. Peper wanted to use an EEG to look for any difference between the function of my brain and that of people who don't evidence any healing ability.

Dr. Peper's experimental setup was similar to Dr. Jampolsky's. Before the test began he attached long, thin cables to several parts of my head. Then I remained in the small lead-shielded room, while he went outside to monitor his equipment. Through an intercom, Dr. Peper told me, successively, to relax, to tense my body and face, and to speak, while he recorded average, or baseline readings. Then he instructed me to enter my healing state and asked me to tell him when I felt I reached a peak healing concentration.

Dr. Peper determined that I had knowledge and control of when I was in a healing state. He also said that my brain waves were "unusual," but that he needed more tests in order to define their significance. Judy promised to contact him to arrange further experiments.

On Wednesday morning Rochelle, Judy and I went to the Stanford University campus to meet Dr. William Tiller, an innovator of research into Kirlian photography in the United States. In the Kirlian process, developed in the Soviet Union, images are produced by electricity, rather than by light. Images are usually made while a subject rests his or her fingertips on the photographic plate, and some researchers believe the resulting picture reveals, graphically, energy emanating from the person's hand.

Dr. Tiller took us to the off-campus home of a friend, where I was to work informally on a few people while hooked up to Kirlian equipment. The treatments went well, but the equipment, although among the finest available, malfunctioned, and Dr. Tiller was unable to obtain a good photograph.

When we returned to the Stanford campus to drop Dr. Tiller off, we unexpectedly encountered Ted Bastin, who had devastating news. He had been discussing the pendulum experiments with Hal Puthoff and Russell Targ, and the physicists had concluded that their controls for the tests had been inadequate. They had managed to stimulate a slight signal, or spike, on the chart recorder by jumping up and down right next to the bell jar and blowing hard on the pendulum case.

This all sounded strange and very unscientific to me, and when I talked later with Hal he admitted that the signals produced by jumping and blowing were by no means as intense as the signals I had produced. He was also well aware that I had been standing quietly ten or more feet from the pendulum. Nevertheless, Hal said, if *any* signal, however small, could be produced artificially, SRI could not support the test results publicly. No papers would be published on the experiment.

I was stunned. I had just begun to understand that this was what it was all about—conducting experiments and publishing the results in respected journals is of the utmost importance to the tiny world of professional parapsychologists. Hal's words filled me with anguish, frustration, and anger.

At Judy's suggestion, we went to the Institute of Noetic Sciences to see Brendan O'Regan, who would probably have more information. One of Brendan's jobs at Noetics was to study experiments in parapsychology and evaluate their feasibility and ramifications, so that the board of directors could choose projects to sponsor.

We found Brendan busily typing. I was nearly frantic as I told him what had happened, and that I wanted to replicate the pendulum experiment immediately. Brendan was sympathetic and tried to calm me, but I insisted that he contact Hal and Russell right away. I had to prove that I could affect their equipment under any controls they could devise. And it had to be tonight, for Rochelle and I were flying home to New York the next morning!

Brendan finally reached Russell, who said it would be impossible to return to the lab that night. Immediately, I offered to extend my stay and return to SRI on Thursday and Friday. But Puthoff's and Targ's schedules were filled for the next few weeks with a study of remote viewing—the ability to perceive distant objects psychically.

I was forced to contemplate a huge failure. SRI, it seemed, was not really prepared to test and measure healing energy or even psychokinesis. In the next few hours, I learned that the pendulum experiment was actually part of the remote viewing experiment—it had nothing to do with the healing research Judy had arranged. It was a confusing and shattering moment.

I seemed to have had a mistaken impression of my California trip. The experiments had been set up very loosely, in part because Judy saw the trip primarily as a get-acquainted visit, a warm-up for further, more intensive studies. If I had understood this from the outset, my disappointment in the test results might not have been so devastating.

That Targ and Puthoff could not write up their findings because of a failure to set up proper controls was aggravating, even more so later on when Puthoff hesitantly confessed to me that as far as he was concerned, I had affected the pendulum apparatus through genuine psychokinesis.

After talking at length with Judy I developed a better understanding of SRI's predicament regarding parapsychological research. SRI—and Targ and Puthoff in particular—had been hurt by the publicity that Uri Geller had attracted, and they were anxious to avoid any further notoriety. In order to maintain its public reputation and its standing in the eyes of the government, which provided so much of its funding, SRI had to be extremely cautious about publishing anything. Still, my understanding did not dispel my disappointment.

I had come to California looking for corroboration of my abilities, expecting that science would provide answers to the many questions I had about my "energy," and it looked like I would be returning home more frustrated than ever. It occurred to me that perhaps I had expected too much from the experiments. I knew I had special "powers"; why were the results of these tests so important to me? Still, I felt angry and sad because my abilities had not been verified.

Before Rochelle and I left for New York, Judy invited several scientists interested in future work with me to come to the Burlingame to get acquainted.

First I met Henry Dakin and Jim Hickman from the Dakin Labs in San Francisco. Impressed by what they had heard about me, they expressed interest in setting up a large-scale research schedule for me in April, five months away. I told them about my unfortunate experience at SRI, but they seemed generally delighted with the results of my trip.

Talking with them made me feel less angry. Then I met a physicist from Lawrence Livermore Laboratories and was even more heartened. He wanted to try to arrange for me to visit the government-affiliated lab to participate in experiments to see whether I could affect human cancer cells in test tubes.

Knowing that I'd be returning to California for a chance to prove myself in more tightly controlled experiments placated my injured feelings and gave me some reassurance. Maybe it was still possible to verify my healing ability and get significant test results published and accepted by the scientific community. I resolved to take a more active part in planning my next trip to California. I especially wanted to know the particulars of the controls on future tests before I undertook them.

My first venture into scientific research had been an education. I hadn't realized before how undeveloped research into healing and ''body energy'' was. Science, I was learning, is suspicious of psychic phenomena, and research into them is so new that scientists tend to be wary. Psychic research is held by most scientists to be an irritating, if not insulting, proposition, not worthy of serious attention or scrutiny. I might have shared such an attitude at one time, but now I was eager—almost desperate—to have my abilities gauged scientifically.

Though the results of my experiments had been a severe disappointment, I had met some good people in the field of parapsychology, and Rochelle and I had found time in San Francisco to reflect on our future and plan our life together. We were grateful to Judy for the trip and only hoped that the next would be more successful. The next time I submitted myself to tests, I'd be much better prepared, mentally and emotionally. All of a sudden, I could hardly wait.

8.

Battling Cancer

As I continued to practice healing I began to appreciate the importance of trying to understand my patients' emotional states as well as their physical states. I found that to "get to" a disease, I couldn't just work on the area that was symptomatic, or the disease might emerge elsewhere in the body. To root out the cause of disease, I have to work with a patient on both a mental and a physical level. In order to do that I have to know and understand the person.

With time, developing this understanding has become somewhat automatic. I ask questions or just pick up things when patients tell me about their illnesses and their history. But understanding goes beyond facts. The more I involve myself with a patient, the more I can love him or her, and love is the essence of healing. In order to help someone I have to feel the patient's situation within myself. I think that empathy may also stimulate my adrenalin and produce a more intense healing effect. Sometimes, if I've wanted to, I've been able to feel someone else's pain.

At the same time I need to maintain a certain distance from the people I heal. It's not the same distance that a physician keeps from a patient; I don't believe my patients feel any distance at all. I feel the need to maintain a psychic distance. Even as I open myself lovingly to my patients, I don't want to open myself to disease or negative mental and emotional conditions.

The most affecting cases I see are cancer cases. I can't help but get caught on an emotional roller coaster when I treat a cancer patient. It's horrifying to get close to somebody and watch him or her go through the ordeal of cancer. If the cancer gets worse I witness the emotional drain on the person, and cancer can pull a whole life down to nothing. Sometimes it gets so bad that I have to detach myself from the situation and let the tension go away. On the other hand, there is no greater joy than seeing a cancer patient start to respond, and hearing from his or her doctors that the patient's improving or that the disease is arrested. Working with cancer patients is like waging war. I feel like I'm battling that son-of-a-bitch cancer, like I'm battling doom.

One cancer patient to whom I grew very close was a man I'll call Dan Morrison, who was referred to me by Judy. Dan, a successful thirty-year-old graphic artist from Vermont, seemed to have a great life— a beautiful wife, three children, property, a good income—but his life had been shattered when his doctors told him he had a brain tumor. The egg-sized growth was in the dominant hemisphere of his brain, and thus inoperable. X rays showed that the tumor was growing, creating more and more intracranial pressure, and therefore precipitating grand mal seizures virtually every day. Doctors had told Dan he had about three months to live.

When I first met Dan, I was surprised at how healthy he looked. Then he self-consciously removed his ski cap and wig for treatment, revealing that radiation therapy, administered in an attempt to shrink the tumor, had left him completely bald. Dan seemed to be in great pain and very frightened.

"I know I have only three months left," he told me sadly that first day. "But I'm just not ready to leave my wife and kids!"

I felt helpless and uneasy, for I couldn't think of anything to say.

Dan's anger and frustration were surfacing. "Damn it!" he cried. "I'm too young to die! I don't want to die yet!"

He told me he'd lost faith in God, and I was pained when he told me how lonely he felt. Unable to face their own fears of death, Dan's friends had virtually abandoned him and his wife.

Wanting desperately to help, I began the treatment. Concentrating on Dan's condition, I saw in my mind a clear and immediate picture, as if I had switched on a television set. I saw an oval tumor in what looked like a spongy substance. Then I saw energy, like shimmering heat waves rising from a burning candle, radiating into the spongy area and into the tumor itself. Then I saw the tumor becoming smaller.

When I finished, Dan told me he had felt as if some activity was in fact taking place in the tumor, though of course he couldn't be sure, especially since he wanted so much to believe I could help him. I too felt certain that I'd made some contact, but the results of Dan's next X rays would be the bottom line. A patient's subjective reports are always important, but not as important as the objective results of medical tests.

I worked with Dan a couple of times a week for the next three weeks, and then he was X rayed. His tumor had decreased to half its original size; the inside of it looked as if it had disintegrated. The doctors were baffled. And Dan's daily seizures were gone.

As I continued to work with Dan we became friends. He was a strikingly intelligent man, very scientifically oriented, and I learned a lot from him. He encouraged me to learn more about traditional medicine. He bought me reference books and urged me to get clinical documentation of my healings. Each time he had an X ray he would explain to me what it revealed.

Over six months Dan's tumor shrunk to a pinhead of scar tissue and Dan was able to return to work. But he stopped seeing Rochelle and me on the friendly, social basis we had established during the time I had worked with him. Every once in a while we'd make a date, but he would always cancel. I took it very personally. I thought perhaps it was because we came from different social strata—Dan was a member of a very wealthy family—and he no longer needed me.

After a few months of silence I received a letter. In it Dan explained that he still loved Rochelle and me, but that seeing me reminded him of the black days when he was planning his funeral and updating his will. Later I spoke with him on the phone, and he was near tears. I still felt a bit hurt, but I understood his need to leave behind the painful memories that had become linked in his mind with me.

Soon, as the result of referrals, half my clients were cancer patients, with every form and in every stage of the disease. Peter Gimbel, the producer of the extraordinarily successful documentary *Blue Water, White Death*, whom I had met socially, came to see me about a small circular growth over his left eyebrow. His doctor had diagnosed the six-month-old growth as a basal cell carcinoma, and a biopsy was scheduled.

Though such growths can generally be treated quite successfully by doctors, Peter was terribly alarmed by the doctor's diagnosis, and my first impulse was to relax his body and mind. Then I worked locally on his forehead. About three days later, Peter called with astonishing news—the small cancerous growth had simply fallen off! It had virtually popped out of his skin. His doctors were stunned that the growth had dislodged itself, but examination showed the skin over Peter's brow to be normal. In a case like Peter's, misdiagnosis might have explained the cure; still, the doctors couldn't explain the sudden disappearance of the growth after so many months.

When Helen Moreno (not her real name) came to me, she had cancer of the cervix, revealed by a cone biopsy, and a fibroid tumor. Her doctors had told Helen, a teacher in her late forties, to prepare herself for a complete hysterectomy. When she and I discussed her illness it emerged that Helen had consulted only one physician and wanted to get a second opinion, so before I even began working with her I referred her to a gynecologist with whom I had worked previously. His diagnosis, however, was the same as that of the first doctor—a complete hysterectomy would give Helen the best chance of recovery.

I began treating Helen, working above the area of her pelvis where the tumor was located and visualizing it decreasing in size. About a month after our first meeting she returned to her doctor at Flower Fifth Avenue Hospital. To his astonishment the fibroid tumor was gone and her Pap smear was normal —there was no longer any need for a hysterectomy.

Adela Spires, whose mother and stepfather, Adela and E. B. Castro, are prominent social figures in San Antonio, Texas, heard about my work from one of the private funders of Stanford Research Institute's parapsychology research. A petite young woman in her early twenties, Adela looked like a skeleton when she was helped into my office by her mother and her aunt, who supported her on either side. Her clothes were hanging off her, and she was so pale that she was almost ghostly. A few months earlier Adela had developed a malignant cyst the size of an orange, and despite surgery, the cancer had spread to her liver. After many operations, chemotherapy, and cobalt treatments, she could hardly walk. She vomited blood nearly every day. Doctors had given up hope—they said Adela had at most three weeks to live—so Adela and her family had traveled from San Antonio, Texas, to Brooklyn, to see me. When I looked at this ashen, bony woman, it seemed her doctors might be right.

I carefully explained to the three women that I had worked with cancer before, sometimes with good results, but that I couldn't promise any improvement. I assured them, however, that I'd do the very best I could for Adela.

With Adela lying on the recliner, I sat behind her, closed my eyes, and blanked out everything around me—the whir of the air conditioner, the soft buzz of voices from the waiting room, the almost palpable anxiety of the two older women. Adela's energy level was so low that she seemed to pull energy out of me. To my own surprise, when the treatment was over Adela prepared to leave without assistance.

Adela and her mother came to the office every day for the rest of the week, and Adela looked better each time. Her yellowed complexion—jaundiced as a result of her liver's involvement in her cancer—was turning a rosier color, and there was a sparkle in her eyes when she told me of the improvements she'd experienced. Her appetite had returned—after our first treatment she could hardly wait to get to a restaurant, where she consumed a cheeseburger, french fries, and a chocolate milk shake. This had impressed Adela's mother most of all, because until then she practically had to force-feed Adela in an attempt to sustain the little strength her daughter had left.

On the last day of the week, Adela, looking wonderful, almost bounced into the office. After the treatment she promised to send me a postcard from Tennessee, where she and her mother were going to vacation. Sure enough, a card arrived the next week. "Thank you," it read. "Having a wonderful time."

Over the next year I conducted several series of treatments on Adela, sometimes in San Antonio, sometimes in New York. I always looked forward to seeing the weight she'd gained, the fullness of her once-gaunt face, and the restored luster of her pale blond hair.

Then Adela's mother called me from a hospital in San Antonio and told me that Adela had just undergone exploratory surgery. I became distraught, but Adela's mother quickly explained that Adela had requested the surgery—she felt strongly that the cancer was gone from her body and she wanted confirmation from her surgeon. Adela's doctor had advised against the operation, for he feared that if there were cancer cells the surgery itself might stimulate their growth and cause them to spread. But Adela had insisted. She had just come out of surgery, and the doctors had found no evidence of cancer.

As Adela's mother spoke I joyfully envisioned Adela fully restored to health and surrounded by her family. I was shocked that Adela had taken such a drastic action, but I had to admit that the results were phenomenal—both for her sake and as a confirmation of her healing.

In mid-July 1977, Adela Spires gave birth to a healthy child, her second. She looked and felt wonderful. And she finally turned a long-held dream into reality—she opened a toy store featuring a selection of unusual, creative toys and rare dolls from around the world. It was always a joy for me to see Adela when she came to New York on a buying trip. The name of her store: I Wish I Wish.

When Joe Titunik helped his sister Helen into my office her body was as wasted as Adela's had been. Her face was gaunt and pale and her eyes were listless. Helen, who was fifty-five, had been stricken with breast cancer, and despite two radical mastectomies the cancer had spread to her liver. She had since undergone repeated chemotherapy, radiation treatments, and surgery, until she was too weak to endure anymore. Medically there was nothing more that could be done for her.

During Helen's first treatment I concentrated only on trying to pump her devastated body as full of "energy" as possible. My objective was to raise her general level of vitality to rid her of fatigue and pain before attempting to work on the cancer itself. And with that very first treatment Helen did seem to gain strength. Later, having read that the lymphatic system is a natural barrier to cancer, I began, in my visualization, to try to energize Helen's lymphatic system.

Helen began coming to see me almost every day, and it quickly became evident to me that she was a very special person. She dealt with the world straight from her heart; she was a loving person who loved for no other motive than for the sake of loving.

After repeated treatments all of us were ecstatic over Helen's increased strength and appetite. Her doctors were puzzled by her wonderful appearance. Ironically, as soon as she grew stronger, they decided that she was again able to endure the effects of chemotherapy. Somewhat hesitantly, Helen agreed. She made it a point to come to me within a day of each chemical treatment, as the chemotherapy left her nauseous, weak, and in pain, and since she was responsive to the "energy" I gave her, I was able to relieve most of the negative effects.

I gave Helen many intensive series of treatments over a five-year period, and eventually repeated blood tests revealed no live cancer cells in her body. As usual when confronted with improvement for which they have no explanation, the doctors labeled her cure a case of spontaneous remission.

I treat Helen every few weeks now, for maintenance. Every time I see her I'm struck again by what a loving and positive person she is. Working with Helen means a great deal to me, because I think having Helen around spreading joy is very important.

Early in 1980 I was called to Lenox Hill Hospital, in Manhattan, to try to help a thirty-eight-year-old woman who was a cancer victim. This was an unusual case for me, for the woman, whom I'll call Sharon Dwyer, was in a coma. Her surgeon thought she might die within hours.

Three years before, I had treated Sharon for a malignant lesion in her eye, and it had disappeared. But now her cancer, which had first developed in her breasts, had metastasized further, spreading throughout her body and into her spine and brain. Before she'd drifted into the coma, increased intracranial pressure had brought on seizures.

I worked with Sharon for two days without getting through. All the nurses knew who I was, and at her husband's and my request, my treatments were noted on Sharon's chart, along with medication, temperature and blood pressure information.

When Sharon's condition continued to decline, her doctor told her husband, Leo, to send for her two children so that they could say good-bye to their mother. Leo called me again, too, although by now all he really hoped was that I'd be able to energize Snaron enough so that she would come out of the coma and see her children.

At the hospital, as I approached Sharon's room, I

saw the chief surgeon emerging from his office. He had been introduced to me previously by Sharon's family, and had accepted my participation in her case very openly. Now he carefully explained Sharon's condition to me. "Look," he concluded, "the fact is that if she can even come out of her coma now it'll be a miracle. So go see what you can do." And he turned and walked down the hall with tears in his eyes, for he had been Sharon's doctor for many years.

Sharon's teenaged daughter and husband were waiting to see her. I asked them to give me about twenty-minutes.

In Sharon's room, I began trying to "pump" her up, counting the minutes till her daughter would enter. I don't do it often, but sometimes when I'm healing I ask for help, and I did so that night. I sort of reached up into the Source or the Soul—whatever there is up there—and said, "Man, I need all the help I can get."

Suddenly it was as if Sharon had been touched by an electric probe. Her body moved abruptly and her eyes opened. It was extraordinary! A moment later Leo ushered in their daughter. He almost passed out when he saw his wife sitting up in bed. Sharon and her daughter threw their arms around one another.

I didn't want her to lose the strength she had gained, so I remained behind Sharon, concentrating on sending energy into her body, while she and her family huddled together, kissing and weeping. I don't know how much my feelings were exaggerated by my physical connection to the group, but I felt myself nearly overwhelmed by emotion.

The next morning the chief surgeon, who had left the hospital before I'd finished treating Sharon, went into her room. He was flabbergasted when slowly and unsteadily but surely, she got out of bed and walked across the room to him.

The day before, X rays made of Sharon's brain tumor had revealed big, dark cancerous lesions. The day after she came out of the coma, new X rays showed that the cancer was gone. Gone! I was accustomed to cancer cases where a tumor grew smaller and smaller over a period of weeks, but this was a real bull's-eye!

Two weeks later Sharon left the hospital, and I traveled to her home and continued to work with her there. On Easter Sunday she got up and walked to the stable to see her horses. She walked slowly, and she still required a full-time nurse, but this was a woman who had been given up for dead less than a month before!

I think that timing is crucial in healing. As a result of my reading and the findings of various tests in which I've participated, I have come to believe that numerous variables—among them, my mental state, the patient's mental state, the position of the moon and sun, the electromagnetic and gravitational forces around the earth—contribute to a healing. These factors all have to line up, like multiple sights on a gun. If they are almost lined up I can get a temporary healing, perhaps, like a six-month remission in a disease. But if all the factors are lined up perfectly, that's when magic can happen. That's how I think Sharon Dwyer was healed.

When a soft-spoken voice teacher from upstate New York—I'll call her Sarah Fisher—began seeing me for treatments, we established a special rapport because of out shared interest in music. Sarah came to me when she was recuperating from a double radical mastectomy. Her surgery had been to no avail, for the surgeons had discovered substantial lymph node involvement in the disease, and the cancer was already spreading to Sarah's lungs and liver.

Because of her radiation treatment and chemotherapy, Sarah was very weak. I was maintaining a hectic schedule, trying to help everyone I could, and sometimes I was called out of town to heal. When I had to leave patients like Sarah I felt distressed and terribly torn. Sarah, who grew to be a close friend, was always advising me to slow down, telling me, "Dean, you can't heal the whole world—you're only one person." One day she brought me a card on which she'd printed a quote from the Talmud: "He who sustains one life is regarded as if he had created the world." The quote helped me gain some perspective on the hectic life I was leading and made me think about the need to pace myself to avoid "burning out" my energy.

During a year of treatment Sarah responded dramatically. Her pain lessened and her breathing difficulties went away. But then she grew sick again and the cancer began to overwhelm her body. I fought the disease as hard as I could, working on her in the hospital as her condition worsened. But this time the miracle I wanted so desperately didn't come.

As Sarah began slipping in and out of consciousness, I felt pulled in two directions. Part of me wanted to revive her and pull her back to life, and another part of me thought of Sarah's suffering and wondered whether in her case death might constitute a true healing.

The last time I laid hands on Sarah I knew her

death was coming. There's a certain thread of life—a little tingle—that I can sense in people, and when I worked with Sarah I didn't feel it anymore.

I learned of Sarah's death from a letter sent by a mutual friend. Although I had expected it, I felt as though I was plunging fifty stories in an elevator car as I read the news. The woman was kind enough to write that Sarah had told her that my healing had alleviated her pain.

Death is a fact of my healing career. When a person I've worked with dies, I feel a personal loss for a time, and then I let it go. I have to, for my own sake. But the loss of Sarah Fisher stayed with me for a long time.

Sarah's case in many ways paralleled that of a man I'll call Carl Woolf. When I first met him, in March 1979, Carl had been fighting multiple myeloma for an unbelievable twelve years, and he was experiencing the roughest period since his illness had struck. Except for an occasional excursion in a wheelchair, he was confined to a hospital bed. His immunological system was at a low ebb, and he was very weak, but his doctors had decided to allow him to go home. They felt he should die in the comfort of familiar surroundings, with his wife, Pam, and eighteen-year-old daughter, Cindy, nearby.

Multiple myeloma is a form of bone cancer that can create multiple fractures and intense pain. Many times Carl would make an ordinary movement and a bone would break. It was rapidly becoming almost impossible for him to move at all. Even his attempts to smile were full of agony. He was depressed by the pain, nausea, appetite loss, and gross weight loss that accompanied his disease, and he told me earnestly that he no longer cared about living.

Before coming to me Carl had tried virtually every available therapy, conventional and unconventional. He had been referred by Dr. Marcy Goldstein, a medical doctor from St. Louis, Missouri, who had practiced plastic surgery before turning to acupuncture and the exploration of other alternate healing methods. Traditional medicine, acupuncture, hypnosis, psychiatry, homeopathy, and chiropractic had not helped Carl. He knew he was dying, and I sensed more readiness than fear on his part.

I focused every bit of energy I could on destroying the cancer cells in Carl's bones, and after several treatments he felt so well that he invited his old card-playing gang to his house and sat for many hours engrossed in playing poker. Carl's attitude also changed, and often he would cry to me that now that he felt so well he didn't want to die.

Soon Carl was able to leave the prison of his bed. At times, to the shock and joy of all, he was able to walk without his wheelchair. His skeletal pain diminished, his appetite improved, and his nausea subsided. He was able to stop taking Percodan, a powerful, toxic, addictive narcotic, after six months of daily use. In the first month I treated him he gained more than seven pounds.

But suddenly, after close to six months of such encouraging progress, Carl took an unexpected turn for the worse. Although I worked with him almost every day, I felt him slipping into his old fatigue and losing his ability to walk. There was one difference from before, though—he had no pain.

Carl eventually reentered the hospital, and soon thereafter he fell into a coma. I held back my tears as I tried desperately to connect with the now-elusive thread of his life. But no matter how intensely I concentrated, I felt Carl slipping away, as though his soul and life force were already beginning to transcend the almost lifeless, diseased mass of brittle bone and thin, pale flesh that was his body.

Suddenly Carl's eyes opened. "My God!" I thought. "He just might be responding. He might be coming out of it!" Carl had tears in his eyes, but there was tranquility in his face. Abruptly stronger, he grabbed my hand, pulled me closer to him and whispered, "God bless you for everything, Dean. It's a wonderful feeling to be ready."

He slipped back into the coma just as suddenly as he'd awakened. His grip loosened and his eyes closed, and I knew I would never see them open again. As I walked out of the hospital room my grief must have been clear to Carl's wife and daughter, and despite her own pain, Pam came over to console me, thanking me for helping Carl to enjoy an extra six months of life. I didn't feel I deserved her gratitude.

As I left the hospital I wondered, as I had in Sarah's case, whether death might be for Carl's benefit. He had been sick a very long time. Still, I felt terribly sad. Though Carl was still alive, I already felt a great sense of loss. Rochelle, waiting to pick me up in our car, took one look at me and knew at once what had happened and what I was going through. She jumped out of the car and ran to embrace me while I cried my heart out.

Carl died peacefully three days later.

One of the great pleasures of my work is to have patients who are recovering from their illnesses come to me exclaiming joyfully, "I'm well! I'm getting well!" But I had become very attached to both Sarah Fisher and Carl Woolf before they died, and in spite of my successes with so many other people, I wasn't able to help them overcome cancer. For some reason, the necessary variables just wouldn't line up. I struggled to help Sarah and Carl, but they didn't get well. I've been given a wonderful gift in healing, but it's not always precisely in my control, not even when it matters most to me.

9.

The Mind-Body Link: Helping Others Help Themselves

My work with cancer patients gave me a dramatic introduction to the role the mind plays in disease. After I had treated many terminal patients I was almost frightened to realize that a common thread ran through every case—each patient had become ill within months of a major emotional upheaval, such as the loss of a loved one or the collapse of a career. Somehow mental and emotional stress had manifested itself in physical illness.

Now new questions hounded me: If the human mind is strong enough to create disease, can the same mind help banish disease and produce good health? What kind of guidance and discipline would enable the mind to achieve this?

Through research I found that some of the preliminary exercises I use to relax myself into a healing state were similar to techniques used in various meditative disciplines. I could find little information on self-healing techniques, however. So I began developing my own theories and methods.

The first task I undertook was to teach patients to relax their bodies and minds in order to release daily tension. I began with a physical relaxation exercise in which I guided patients through the progressive relaxation of every body part, instructing them to tense and release each area from their toes up through their forehead and temples.

Then I explained how they could relax their minds as well as their bodies, as I believe that when the body and mind are synchronized in a relaxed state, a person is more able to channel the energy within himself. For mental relaxation, I taught a technique requiring visualization. I explained that visualization is vivid imagining—seeing, not with the eyes, but on the blank screen of the mind. After my patients had relaxed physically I instructed them to visualize a body of water, and to see the water as calm and as smooth as possible. All other thoughts were ripples in that smooth, glasslike lake, and the goal was to smooth out the lake as much as possible, eliminating all other thoughts. The fewer thoughts in the mind, the more it could relax.

Other times I had patients visualize a burning candle and try to hold the flame as steady as possible. The more thoughts that came into their mind, the more the flame would flicker; the calmer the mind, the stiller the flame. The particular visualization didn't matter—the important thing was to deal with as few thoughts as possible.

To develop the actual self-healing exercises I began by experimenting on myself. I chose as my point of concentration a small growth that I'd had on my right index finger for several years. I lay down on a couch and relaxed my mind and body, and immediately, on the blank screen of my mind, I began to see a bright blue light moving around my body. At the same time I felt heat, which moved with the light. In my mental picture I was seeing myself from a height of about eight feet, looking down at an angle at the couch where I lay. The blue light moved around the perimeter of my body, beginning at my head and moving down my left side, in a clockwise direction. The light and heat seemed propelled by my breathing; as I inhaled the light moved slowly, and as I exhaled it moved more rapidly.

I was amazed as I watched the illumination grow wider and more vibrant when it reached the growth on my hand. My finger actually felt warmer, almost hot, as the brilliant light passed over it. The light circled my body several times, and each time it went over my finger it widened and intensified. After about fifteen minutes I felt satisfied with my attempt. I repeated this exercise several times over the next few days, and by the end of the week the growth was gone.

I tried out this combination of relaxation and self-healing exercises on several friends and a few interested doctors, and I was encouraged when several of them reported positive results. In particular, the exercises seemed to enable people to alleviate their own pain. Thereafter I taught the techniques to most of my clients, because I didn't want them to feel entirely dependent on me for help. In 1976 I developed self-healing seminars for the public. The first, in Brooklyn, drew more than two hundred people, and I followed it with seminars in Manhattan and then in Houston, Texas.

The question of whether the ability to heal other

people can be taught is of even greater interest to most people than self-healing. But, as yet, I don't know the answer.

In 1976 I lectured at a Grand Rounds meeting at Lincoln Hospital in the Bronx. The lecture was arranged by Dr. David Laskowitz, a prominent psychologist at the hospital, who had heard me speak on the radio. I was honored to give the monthly lecture, which is intended to keep hospital doctors up to date on new research and general medical information, and is usually delivered by a physician. I knew my talk had gone well when Dr. Michael O. Smith, director of the drug detoxification program at Lincoln, approached me to ask whether my methods could be taught. His interest finally prompted me to develop a step-by-step technique for the laying on of hands that others could follow.

It was very difficult for me to dissect the process that had become so automatic to me, but when I had done so the method I had outlined in many ways paralleled the self-healing techniques I had developed. First I led would-be healers through the process of relaxing their own bodies and minds. Then I instructed them to lightly place their thumbs together on the patient's mid-forehead, forming a triangle above the eyes. (I now know that this area is known as "the third eye" and plays an important role in Eastern theories of body energy, but I discovered it instinctively; when I began healing I often found myself focusing on this area.)

Next I instructed healers to visualize a connection between themselves and the sick person, and to feel themselves sending their own energy into the sick person's body. I told them to imagine light and heat, propelled and controlled by their own slow breathing, circling the ill person's body and expanding in width as it passed over afflicted areas. After each cycle around the ill person, the energy was to be drawn back to the healer, then sent out again to the recipient.

When I first started healing I had seen light going around. As I did more healing the process became more automatic; I felt energy going around without seeing it, and my visualization was concentrated on the pathology itself. But the healing method I had outlined was a simple version of my own technique.

I presented this method to Dr. Smith, and we arranged for my return to the hospital to begin teaching the laying on of hands to the doctors in charge of the detoxification program. I showed several physicians and medical assistants how to place their hands on the patient's mid-forehead and concentrate on trying to stimulate health while lessening pain, anxiety, and depression. The doctors seemed pleased with the session, and so was I, and Dr. Smith told *The London Daily Mail* that the detox unit uses my techniques regularly.

For those who are skeptical about psychic healing, one justification for teaching doctors the laying on of hands is that it may increase their sensitivity and lead them to give their patients a little more tender loving care. Many doctors I've talked with have told me that warm, caring treatment is notably lacking in modern medical practice.

What's most needed now is controlled research to determine whether people trained in the laying on of hands can actually heal other people or do any form of demonstrable psychokinesis; to see if they can create a measurable physical effect. I think I can teach other people to create a real healing effect, but to what degree I don't know. My guess is that I can find some sensitive people who can develop their natural abilities with guidance. The right attitude will be an important attribute in potential healers, for true healing is not involved with ego. It depends on the healer's desire to be loving and to help the sick person.

When evidence of healing by the laying on of hands is presented to skeptics, they most commonly respond that the healing is the result of suggestion, or the "placebo effect." But recent research into the relationship of mind and body has made it more difficult for scientists to dismiss the phenomenon lightly.

According to the theory of the placebo effect, if a doctor gives one hundred patients who complain of pain a simple sugar pill, he can be sure that thirty-three will feel better. Until recently the effect has been attributed to psychological factors. But studies conducted in the last few years have suggested that inert placebo pills actually have physical effects after all.

A variety of experiments have shown that after a subject is given a placebo a physiological change takes place in the brain, which produces opiatelike substances called endorphins. These natural brain chemicals are one of the body's own painkillers. Perhaps more powerful than any available medication, they act on specific receptors in the brain and spinal cord just as morphine and other narcotics do. Other studies have shown that additional substances are also produced by the brain in response to the stimulus of a placebo.

If a placebo can cause the brain to create substances that alleviate pain, a similar model may be at work in the effectiveness of all healing techniques, including Western medicine, hypnosis, acupuncture, chiropractic, homeopathy, and psychic healing.

That is not to say that I affect most of the people I heal through a placebo effect. I think it's more likely that science will ultimately find that I am somehow able to alter the force fields around the living cells. But a certain percentage of people, who respond to any therapy, including traditional medicine, do so as a result of the placebo effect.

Even if psychic healing is *just* a placebo or works *just* by suggestion (and I don't think that's the case), psychic healing is beneficial. If suggestion is so effective, then why deny "hopeless" cases its possible benefits? Why do doctors continually discourage patients, telling them there's absolutely nothing more that can be done for them?

I have always felt that as long as an alternate healing method does not harm a patient, there is no reason for doctors, family, or friends to discount it, especially if doctors have given up hope. When medical procedures have been exhausted, why should anyone object to trying other approaches? The only reason I can think of is doctors' egos; if they can't help, they think no one and nothing else can.

Many doctors argue that they don't think it is fair to raise the hopes of terminally ill patients. But I believe hope is the very first thing that should be administered in any circumstance. As long as one is honest and doesn't promise to perform miracles, a patient has nothing to lose—and may have life and health to gain. With hope comes the will to live.

10.

Scientific Testing: A Successful Second Round

We were back in San Francisco.

It was Tuesday, April 15, 1975, five o'clock in the morning, and I was lying in the spacious bed at the Burlingame Hyatt House, looking on with envy as Rochelle slept. I couldn't sleep anymore; my mind wouldn't rest. The rising sun signaled that my second attempt at scientifically proving my healing abilities was about to begin. In a few hours I'd begin a tenday battery of tests, which I hoped would result in more definitive information than the first tests I had undergone. I felt the pressure on me steadily increasing.

Submitting myself to the tests was not a selfless act for the benefit of science. *I* was curious. I still needed answers to the same old questions: Did I in fact produce energy that healed? What kind of energy was it? Where did it come from? Why me? I was sure that the better I understood the energy, if that was what it was, the better I would be able to direct it to help people with their illnesses.

I also wanted to learn all I could about the equipment, procedures, and controls utilized in proper research into parapsychological phenomena. Since our disappointing first visit to California, Rochelle and I had begun to discuss the possibility of establishing our own research foundation. I hoped that during this trip I would learn enough so that when the time came, I'd be able to guide my own organization into accurate and useful healing research.

The alarm clock shocked me out of my reverie.

Through Judy's intercession, this trip had been underwritten by Henry Dakin, a wealthy electrophysicist and inventor, who had paid Rochelle's and my airfare, a fee for my time, and fees to a variety of labs and academic institutions that would be participating in the study. Henry was one of a close-knit group of scientists who worked with Judy and the Institute of Noetic Sciences in testing sensitive subjects. Several years before, he had converted his old brownstone house, situated in one of the lovely residential sections of San Francisco, into a highly sophisticated, multifloored laboratory for parapsychology research and for the development of his own inventions. Today was my orientation day at Dakin Laboratories; the tests would begin tomorrow.

Assistant researchers Jim Hickman and Roger Macdonald, both about thirty, gave Rochelle and me a tour of the lab. Then Henry Dakin, a gray-haired man in his late forties, greeted us. Henry was pleasant but somewhat distant, as though he was preoccupied with other business, and Jim didn't seem as open and eager as he had when I met him during my first California trip. They both were polite, but seemed to be holding me at arm's length. At first I thought it was their way of maintaining scientific objectivity, but later Judy told me that Dakin had been annoyed and upset about some recent articles published about me, particularly one in a sensational tabloid. Judy advised me to ignore Jim's and Henry's coolness, for she believed publicity was important in educating the public. I just hoped their attitudes wouldn't affect the publication of any test results.

As Jim, Roger, Rochelle and I walked through the corridors of Dakin Labs, Jim explained some of the experiments involved in our study. The project was called "Preliminary Physical Measurements of Psychophysical Effects Associated with Three Alleged Psychic Healers." Also participating in the study were healers Olga Worrall and the Reverend John Scudder. Reverend Scudder had already completed his tests and Mrs. Worrall would be tested after me.

A number of the experiments would attempt to replicate work done previously by notable parapsychology researchers. Some of these replications were to deal with electric and magnetic field variations; others with plant growth, brain-wave measurements, and molecular changes in water. The researchers at Dakin wanted to use some of Dakin's specially designed instruments in the replications and wanted to set up testing conditions that were the same or better than those used in the original experimental designs.

As our first day at Dakin Labs drew to a close Jim and Roger handed me the schedule for the next nine days. Some of my tests would be conducted elsewhere—at a number of government- and university-affiliated research centers and institutes in the area. Some of them demanded anonymity because of the controversial nature of the work. The next day included brain-wave work at Stanford Research Institute, experiments with the growth of bacteria at a San Francisco research and development company, and an experiment on a hypertensive laboratory rat at a medical institute. The rest of the week I'd be based at Dakin Labs. The following week would include an experiment with cancer cells at Lawrence Livermore Laboratories. It would be a heavy work load, but I felt ready. Back at the hotel that night I went to sleep feeling eager and enthusiastic.

Wednesday morning Rochelle and I were driven to SRI. Though I would not be seeing Targ and Puthoff on this trip, I was going to work again with Dr. Erik Peper of the biomedical department. He was again going to monitor my brain waves and those of a volunteer "patient" during a healing session. He hoped that a correlation between my "healing state" and brain-wave patterns could be established.

Dr. Peper explained that I would treat the volunteer in an electrically shielded room, which was separated from the room where the scientists monitored their machines by what looked like a two-foot-thick refrigerator door. In the "treating room," both the volunteer and I would be wired to an EEG, she reclining in a lounge chair and I sitting in a club chair behind her. Jim Hickman would remain in the room as an observer. Rochelle and Roger Macdonald would be allowed to observe from the outer room.

Dr. Peper, Jim, and I chatted while they started the long and messy procedure of attaching the EEG wires to different parts of my head with white paste. Then Dr. Peper introduced the volunteer and attached wires to her head in the same way. We were given careful instructions. If during the session I felt

I had reached a peak in my healing state, I was to press a button on the chair arm to indicate this to Peper. If the woman felt herself in a state of unusually deep relaxation, she was to press a similar button.

Dr. Peper showed us an intercom system that would enable us to communicate with him once he went into the next room. Then he and Macdonald exited and closed the thick door, leaving, Jim, the volunteer, and me in the treating room.

Over the intercom Dr. Peper told us to go on chatting casually—he wanted to record our normal, or baseline, brain waves. Then he told me to begin the actual healing. I automatically sank deeper into a relaxed state and focused on a general relaxation treatment for the volunteer. Gradually I felt myself achieving a balance between my mind and my body—I felt blissful. Then I remembered the button. Removing one hand from the woman's shoulder I pushed the button, though it was distracting, and I felt I lost some of the intensity I'd been building up.

During the session I noticed that the volunteer pushed her own button several times. Occasionally Dr. Peper announced over the intercom that my brain waves were changing, and I'd concentrate harder on maintaining a steady peak state. Dr. Peper ran several trials with rest periods in between.

After the test was over Dr. Peper scanned the chart recorder's printed output, comparing the volunteer's chart with mine. At several points our brain-wave patterns were strikingly synchronized, he told us. It also appeared that when I pressed the buzzer to indicate that I was in my most concentrated healing state, the EEG recorded alpha waves—those associated with a deep, meditative state. Dr. Peper was excited about these preliminary findings and suggested to Jim and Roger that I come back the following week for more tests.

Then we were on our way to the next location, the research and development company where an experiment would be conducted to see if I could affect the growth rate of bacteria. The company had never dealt with parapsychologists before, and the attitude of their personnel reflected that fact; the scientists were almost hostile to Jim, Roger, Rochelle, and me. I decided not to let their attitude bother me.

Our group was led into a testing room and two trays were brought in. Each held twenty-four sealed vials: eight vials each of two strains of soil bacteria, and eight of a strain of intestinal bacteria. One tray of vials would serve as the control group, and I would attempt to affect the contents of the vials on the other.

With Jim, Roger, Rochelle, and a representative of the research center observing from the opposite end of the room, I was seated at a long table with the large tray of bacteria in front of me. I was told I could hold my hands at the sides of the tray, over the top, or in any other position I thought might produce results. When I asked if I could be contaminated by the bacteria, I was assured that the experiment was safe.

I picked up one vial and held it to the light, trying to get a good look at my "subject," but the container was opaque. I asked if there were any clear plastic containers, but the answer was no. Thus I had nothing to visualize during the session, but I did the best I could. At the end of twenty minutes I knew I hadn't made a mental connection with the bacteria. I told the researchers the difficulty I'd experienced.

The observing techinician took an experimental and control sample from the room to run them through a bacteria counter. We watched him discuss the samples with another technician, and then he returned and took another vial to analyze. Then, although the experiments at the research center had been scheduled to run for several days, the company suddenly canceled the remaining sessions, explaining that they had decided not to do any more psychic research. We never would discover the reason for their sudden change of heart.

We were all bewildered by this abrupt dismissal, but we had little time to dwell on it, for we were due at a medical institute, where we joined Dr. Jerry Jampolsky and Judy Skutch. As we were about to enter this impressive research center, Jerry explained to me that the research director, whom I'll call Dr. Vickers, had requested that there be no observers around the lab. So Judy, Rochelle and Jim took off to tour the city, while Jerry, Roger, and I went into the institute.

When the three of us entered Dr. Vicker's office, he greeted us with a pronounced lack of enthusiasm. He briskly led us to the lab that had been set aside for our use, pointed to a Plexiglas cage containing the experimental subject—a laboratory rat—and introduced us to two lab technicians, before making a hasty exit.

By now I was growing accustomed to such treatment from scientists, and Vickers's lack of interest didn't bother me a bit. Curiously I walked over to the Plexiglas cage, looked inside, and saw a huge white rat with a long, skinny tail. I had known in advance that I'd be working with a rat, but somehow I hadn't expected it to look so repulsive and frightening.

Anxiously I said, "Jerry, I'm not sure I'm going to be able to do this."

I tried to explain that my only previous experience with rats had been in the music store, where foot-long rats that lurked in the basement sometimes ventured upstairs and scared the hell out of everybody. I felt only hate and fear for rats, and I was worried, for it had always seemed to me that I needed to have positive thoughts—loving thoughts—toward the subjects I tried to heal.

Jerry tried to relieve my distress by talking, outlining the object of the experiment. I was to try, by means of my energy, to lower the blood pressure of this rat, one of a strain that, otherwise healthy, had been bred specifically for hypertension. The rat's blood pressure and pulse rate would be continually monitored and recorded.

As Jerry checked my own blood pressure before the experiment I again stressed my trepidation and distaste. I knew I couldn't back out of the test, but I wanted to be sure the researchers knew that I doubted my ability to succeed with a subject that generated such negative feelings. If they understood that, I was willing to do my best. Indeed, I was curious, for I'd never worked on an animal before.

Before the test began I asked if I could be given feedback during the experiment—I wanted to be informed if I was in fact affecting the rat's blood pressure. During the earlier experiment at SRI with Dr. Peper I had found that when Peper reported changes in my brain-wave pattern over the intercom, the information somehow enabled me to raise my energy level still higher. If Peper's feedback indicated no change of pattern, I had worked harder to produce a larger energy output.

An oscilloscope—a device with a screen on which the rat's pulse rate could be monitored visually—was put within my view. A declining pulse rate would accompany declining blood pressure. The rat's normal pulse rate was already displayed, as wavy horizontal lines.

When I got the go-ahead from Jerry, I began to concentrate, placing my hands several inches above the see-through enclosure and closing my eyes, for I was truly repulsed by the rat. No matter how I tried I couldn't seem to muster up any love. I didn't feel that I could open up to the rat and make a good connection. For twenty minutes I tried to lower the rat's blood pressure, but each time I glanced at the oscilloscope the pattern was unchanged.

Suddenly Jerry murmured, "The pulse rate is going down."

I turned to observe the screen again—all eyes were glued to it now—and saw the lines descending. But Jerry was so intent on watching the screen that without realizing it, he turned the oscilloscope out of my view.

I began to concentrate even more diligently on lowering the rodent's blood pressure. When I asked for someone to tell me whether the rat's pulse rate was still dropping or if its blood pressure had begun to drop, no one answered. I worked for another ten minutes in the suddenly silent room, then stopped.

I felt that something was wrong, a bit off, but I couldn't put my finger on it. I was taken into a different room, where Jerry rechecked my own blood pressure, which was normal. He told me to stay there, and left. When he returned with Roger and the technicians their faces bore a mixture of excitement and fascination that I couldn't interpret. Then Dr. Vickers came in, flanked by two more scientists. Suddenly friendly, Dr. Vickers put his arm around my shoulders and asked for my subjective impression of the experiment. I told him that I hadn't been able to shake my distaste for the rat, and that after about twenty minutes I had felt something begin to happen, but that I wasn't sure what it was.

Dr. Vickers then asked me what kind of animals I did like. I probably shouldn't work with rats, he said, in a tone that implied a joke—maybe rabbits would be better. I couldn't figure out the point of all this banter.

Finally Jerry interrupted, "Dr. Vickers, don't you think we should tell him?"

And Vickers, still smiling, sat down and told me the results of the test: "Dean," he said, "the rat you worked on is dead."

I felt my heart leap.

"Approximately twenty minutes after you began to work on the rat, it died," Vickers went on. "Its blood pressure was so low that its heart stopped."

I was confused. I could see how intrigued the researchers were, but my own reaction was frustration —if only they had given me more feedback on the rats blood pressure, as I had asked, I would have stopped working sooner. I hadn't wanted to kill the poor rat. I felt disgusted, tired, confused.

As we discussed the results of the test, however, I began to understand its implications. It was a little frightening to think that I could have brought on the rat's death. But the new scientific side of me was also fascinated to think that my fear and loathing of the rat might have led to its death.

My energy, I supposed, must coordinate with my attitude. I reassured myself, remembering that though I hadn't always personally liked the people I'd treated I'd always felt a loving connection during sessions.

A postmortem examination would be conducted to see if the exact cause of the rat's death could be determined, the scientists told me. The statistical chance of sudden death in that breed of rat under such experimental conditions would be determined.

When Roger and I returned to Dakin Labs to pick up Rochelle and Judy, they and the Dakin staff were thrilled by our account of the rat experiment. But I was thoroughly exhausted by the unsettling events of the day.

Rochelle and I slept late the following morning, for we had the day to ourselves until after dinner. In the evening several representatives of Lawrence Livermore Laboratories met with us, Judy, and Bob Williamson in Bob's room. The scientists wanted to discuss the upcoming work with cancer cells.

The scientists quickly explained the point of the scheduled experiment: They wanted to see if I could affect a culture of cancer cells in test tubes. They had brought a film of the microscopic cells, enlarged several thousand times, so that I could see what I'd be dealing with. It was the most aggressive type of cancer cell known to science—named HeLa, for Henrietta Lacks, a young black woman who died of cervical cancer in 1951. Cancer had run rampant through her body, and when she died cell cultures of the disease had been preserved and nurtured so that scientists could conduct experiments on the unusually virulent cells. Medical researchers around the world utilize HeLa cells in the search for a cancer cure.

We watched the film of the squirmy, oval cells taken as they were about to multiply; approximately every twenty-four hours each cell splits into two separate cells. The scientists were looking for any change at all—the breakdown of the adhesive culture, a speeding up or slowing down of reproduction—in the cells or their activity. I was frightened by the idea of working with cancer cells, and I asked about the chance of the disease being transmitted to me. I was told it was highly unlikely, but I didn't really feel reassured.

I was to begin work on the cells on Monday. The Livermore scientists told me that if I detected any hostility from any of the other researchers at the lab I should ignore it. It had been difficult to arrange my visit to Lawrence Livermore, where most researchers were opposed to parapsychology research.

The next day, Friday, as Rochelle and I were leaving our hotel room to go to Dakin Labs, we got a call from Dr. Jampolsky about the rat experiment. Examination of the dead animal had provided absolutely no explanation for its death. There had been no cerebral hemorrhage, no seizure—the rat's heart had simply stopped. Dr. Vickers had also done a quantitative and qualitative statistical analysis and determined that no other rodent had ever died in such a way in a Plexiglas cage.

After this exciting call we went on to the lab. Jim Hickman took us into a room, sat me down, and handed me what looked like a bottle of water. It was actually a bottle of saline solution, and he wanted me to concentrate on transmitting my energy to it. The solution would then be used to water some rye seeds, and their rate of growth would be observed. A plant watered with saline solution would be expected to be sickly, and the scientists wanted to see if I could overcome the negative effect of the saline solution by energizing the solution by the laying on of hands.

I suddenly realized that Roger wasn't around, and asked Jim where he was. Roger would not witness the treatment of the solution, Jim said. In the second part of the experiment, Roger would water the seeds—some with the solution I treated and some with a control solution. It was a "blind" experiment, meaning Roger wouldn't know which bottle was which.

I felt rather silly treating the bottle of solution. I would have preferred to work directly with the plants or seeds, for it seemed a lot easier to "love" them.

It would be two months after I left California before I learned the results of the plant growth experiment. Then I was notified that I had significantly altered the growth of the plants. Those watered with the unhealthy solution I had treated had grown more slowly than those in the control group, but they had been healthy.

After I finished treating the saline solution I was escorted to the chilly basement, where a room was equipped with Kirlian photography equipment designed by Henry Dakin. Roger showed me examples of Kirlian photographs that showed colored flares, some like bursts of fire, issuing from fingertips.

Experimental photos of my hands would be taken when I indicated that I was in a healing state, Jim said, and control photos would be taken when I was not concentrating. I was concerned that I'd have to break my concentration in order to signal the researchers that I was in a deep meditative state, just as I'd had to disrupt my concentration to ring the buzzer in Dr. Peper's experiment. We worked out the best system that we could: Jim would sit next to me, and when I felt deeply relaxed I'd press my knee against his, and he'd make a picture.

After several tests Roger developed the film, and he and Jim said they detected some interesting flares emerging from my hands, but that they would have to analyze them further. Knowing that some dramatic early experiments involving Kirlian photography and healers had not been successfully replicated under strict controls, I asked if Jim and Roger believed that the flares revealed by Kirlian photography really represented energy emanating from the body. I wasn't too surprised when they said they couldn't be sure. Because so many factors—dirt on the fingers, varied pressure on the film plate, changing temperature—could affect the patterns shown in the photographs, they could not make any conclusive statement about the phenomenon, except that someday it might be a very useful tool.

At the conclusion of the Kirlian experiment, Jim and Roger showed me to the next room, which held the machinery for what they considered to be one of the major parts of our study. On the left was a huge see-through structure of wire mesh, called a Faraday cage. Easily large enough to accommodate fifteen standing adults, the enclosure was designed so experiments could be conducted in a location free of radio waves or magnetic fields; the cage minimized the effect of interference from power lines and radio stations. The purpose of our experiment was to determine if I could produce changes in the electrostatic field within the cage with my own energy.

During the experiment I would sit inside the Faraday cage with my hands resting palms upward on a lapboard. A square metal box would generate an electrostatic field inside the cage in the area above my hands. The generator was connected by cable to an oscilloscope linked to a chart recorder and a tone feedback system, all located outside the cage. If there were any disturbances in the electrostatic field inside the cage the steady tone of the feedback system would change pitch and the chart recorder would record the degree to which the field was affected.

All of the equipment inside the cage was so sensitive that movement of any kind could invalidate the tests. Video cameras would be trained on me to assure that I remained prefectly still. Before the experiment began I was instructed to take my seat inside the cage, remove my shoes, roll up my pants legs, and place my hands on the lapboard. My pockets were checked for metal. Then I was asked to move my hands in the vicinity of the metal box, while the movement was noted on the chart recorder as an "artifact." In turn, I was told to move my head, my legs, and my toes, and to breathe deeply, so that during the experiment, if any movement was recorded in the cage, the record could be compared with the body "artifacts" already transcribed.

Finally everything was in order. Jim, Roger, and an assistant in charge of the video cameras explained that I was to have sixteen trials. Each trial would be comprised of three parts: for forty-five seconds of "experiment" I was to concentrate on affecting the field with my own energy; for forty-five seconds of "control" I was not to affect the field, and for fifteen seconds I was to rest. They would not say in advance which part of the trial they would call for. Jim would randomly say, for example, "forty-five seconds experiment," and, as quickly as I could, I would begin to generate energy in an attempt to disturb the electrostatic field being produced inside the cage.

This was going to be fun! I knew I had the control of my energy that they were searching for and could turn "on" for the experimental period and "off" for the control and rest periods. Indeed, once we began, each time I was given the command for "experiment," I would visualize energy rising from my hands like heat waves toward the metal box, and the feedback tone would instantly change pitch. I remember watching Rochelle standing with Jim and Roger, excitedly watching the oscilloscope and chart recorder. Apparently the readings sometimes went so high that Roger had to turn down the dials. Each time I concentrated and the field showed changes Roger would start to yell, "Yeah! Yeah," and jump up and down with excitement. Then he'd check with the camera person to be certain that I hadn't moved.

When we left for the weekend Rochelle and I were tired but happy. Throughout the two days off I tried to relax and have fun, but my thoughts kept drifting to Monday and the coming experiment with the cancer cells. Exposure to cancer was still frightening to me, and I was very nervous. But come Monday the Livermore staff was still working on the design of the HeLa experiment, and work was postponed till Friday.

For the next three days I repeated the Faraday cage experiment at Dakin Labs with the same tight controls. I affected the field significantly during every trial every day. The experiments were going so well that the atmosphere was giddy; Jim and Roger would cheer me on.

I also participated in more brain-wave experiments. A researcher at a major medical center, testing for possible correlations of the brain waves of healer and healee, came up with findings similar to those of Dr. Peper at SRI. There were moments of synchronicity, and my brain waves during healing exhibited a very deep alpha state. Dr. Peper also did more EEG recordings, and once again his findings were unusual—"intriguing," he said. He wanted to arrange for a full week of testing in the future.

Before I knew it Friday arrived, and it was time to try to alter the HeLa cancer cells. I was so high from the successes I'd already enjoyed during the trip that the HeLa experiment just seemed like something extra, and I was now very relaxed about it. I had finally convinced myself that I could hold the flask of cancer cells without contracting a fatal disease.

When I arrived at Livermore Labs I was subjected to elaborate security checks and given a pass to wear at all times. I was dressed in lightweight cotton clothes and I had brought along a short-sleeve T-shirt to wear, for I would be working in the "sweatbox"— an incubator room where the temperature was maintained at 98.6 F. and there was only a narrow walkway between two walls that held countless flasks of cancer cells.

The researcher in charge of the experiment, whom I'll refer to as Richard, brought in a "double-eyed" microscope that would permit us to observe the cancer cells simultaneously before and after the experiment. Pointing to another flask of cells on a shelf Richard explained that it was the control and would not be touched by me or anybody. He then departed for a meeting, leaving an assistant to monitor the experiment while I concentrated for half an hour on affecting the cells.

Perhaps I was still troubled by fear, for I felt absolutely no interaction develop. We took a lunch break, and I began working again. After about twenty minutes of deep concentration I began to feel a repulsion between my hands and the flask. It was remarkable—it felt as though the cancer cells were resisting me! Then, suddenly, I felt the pressure collapse, as if some of the cells had stopped pushing. As if they had surrendered.

Tremendously excited, I motioned to the assistant and asked her to check the cells. Then she got very excited, for there did seem to be a lot of cells floating on top of the solution, many more than before I began to work on them. As minutes passed, more "floaters" (dead cells) surfaced—the cells were breaking up! I was ecstatic.

When Richard returned from his meeting he also examined the cells. He and his assistant went into separate rooms to write up their visual observations, then compared them and found them quite similar. Richard was obviously shaken.

We were joined by another scientist. He too observed the cells, but his response was that if you shook the flasks you could get the same result. The assistant immediately took one of the control flasks and shook it vigorously, but the cells remained unaffected.

For yet another opinion Richard called in a biologist, who seemed very reluctant to even get involved with what we were doing. He looked into the experimental and control flasks and reported emphatically that he saw no difference between them. This bothered Richard, for he and his assistant had both noted a definite difference between the flask I had worked on and the control. So we all went into another lab, where Richard put the cells through a Coulter Counter, a machine that could count the number of floating cells in a sample. The number of floaters in the control was approximately 530; the number in the flask I had worked on, was approximately 1,200—more than twice as many! The biologist, who was still with us, was taken aback and he said he'd like to run the test himself. He did, and the results were the same.

I felt just great. I had caused cancer cells to break apart! No one in the lab had ever seen such a thing happen before. I felt there was nothing that I couldn't do, and, of course, the test results confirmed me in my work with cancer patients.

In addition, the information about my abilities revealed by the experiments in which I'd participated pointed to a possible healing mechanism. The Faraday cage experiment had shown that I could alter an electrostatic field, and an informal test with a magnetometer I had apparently affected a magnetic field. This suggested to me that perhaps I had been able to affect the HeLa cells by altering the electromagnetic force field that research has shown surrounds all cells, and that a similar model is at work in my healing of living people.

While acknowledging that I had affected the cell cultures, Richard cautioned me not to get carried away. Still, his own excitement was evident and contagious as he started planning a larger-scale series of tests for July. I asked him for a written report, and he said he would mail me one within a week.

The following day, when Rochelle and I returned to New York, I was floating. Before doing any experiments I had known that I was a good healer. But the experiments had shown that not only could I heal, but I could demonstrate at least some of my ability scientifically. I had proved that something, though still unexplained, really happened when I healed.

I was even more gratified a year later, when a report on the healing experiments conducted under the direction of Dakin Labs was submitted as a "research brief" to the Parapsychology Association for its conference in Utrecht, Holland. All in all, I felt very satisfied with the research conducted during my second California trip, and content that I was finally getting closer to finding the answers to what my healing was all about.

11.

In the Public Eye

After I began my career as a healer, my first tastes of publicity—the radio programs and newspaper articles—were a great boost to my ego. After all, I'd come out of the music business, where fame is inherent in everyone's goals. Then Judy Skutch instilled in me a firm respect for publicity as a way of communicating new and controversial concepts to the public.

One of the most memorable early articles about me was published on December 23, 1974, in *The Village Voice,* a famous New York weekly. The front page of the paper carried a picture of me demonstrating my healing technique on Rochelle. A huge headline read, "The Brooklyn Healer," and in smaller letters were the words, "Why the Psychics Are Betting on This Man."

Coming as it did on the heels of my disappointing first trip to California in search of acceptance for my work, the appearance of the article marked a glorious moment for Rochelle and me. We read the lengthy piece together, overjoyed to see how carefully written and accurate it was. The reporter, who had heard of me through Judy Skutch, surprised us with the thoroughness of his portrayal, which reported the events of my life up to that time and stressed the importance of my ability to demonstrate my powers in the laboratory.

The best part of the article were interviews with several of my clients who had gone on the record about my work with them. Yoko Ono told how she had seen me perform PK in her apartment; a New York family court judge confirmed that after my treatments he had experienced no more arthritis pain; even Dr. Jampolsky, from California, acknowledged that my brain-wave patterns showed more alpha waves than one would expect.

The same week, the article John Peterson had written about my treatment of his knee tumor appeared in *The National Observer*. That story, very conservative and low keyed, was titled "I'm Not Always Successful," a quote from me, and was a fine account of our session together.

I was delighted with the *Voice* and *Observer* articles, which I thought would lend credibility to parapsychology as well as to me personally. I didn't anticipate that they would set off a virtual avalanche of secondary publicity. *Cosmopolitan* soon reprinted the *Voice* article, and suddenly newspapers, radio, and television shows were fascinated with me—an ordinary guy who practices the laying on of hands without long robes or mumbo jumbo.

It was flattering, of course, to be the object of so much attention, and after a few shows I even began to enjoy the nervous tension that accompanied an appearance on TV or radio. There were times, though, when I wondered what it all really meant for me, and—more important—for my work. I knew that the media are fickle; they leap on something or someone novel, then skitter quickly to the next new phenomenon. Meaning and substance are sometimes less important than filling hours on the air with something unusual.

After I had appeared on many programs and been widely written up, I was distressed to realize that psychic healers usually considered in the same group with crystal ball gazers and astrologers. I found it frustrating when a reporter or talk show host confused my nonreligious, scientifically oriented work with that of a spiritual healer.

Within a week of the publication of the *Voice* article, I appeared on *The Pat Collins Show* on CBS, and the response was so terrific that I was invited back the following month. The second time, Judy Skutch, well-known faith healer Ethel DeLoach, and writer-physician William Nolen were also on the show. Nolen had recently published a book, *Healing: In Search of a Miracle,* which was an account of his search for a case of true healing by such faith healers as the late Kathryn Kuhlman and Norbu Chen. His conclusion was that there was no evidence of people being cured by healers.

As I listened to Dr. Nolen I realized that he had only investigated healers who had never sought scientific validation of their work. I asked if he'd ever thought about studying a healer who had subjected himself to medical and scientific testing. Would he consider investigating me? Nolen acknowledged that his search had not included anyone who had sought acceptable means of establishing his or her healing abilities. And while he declined to investigate me, thus confronted, he did say that he thought healing powers do exist, but that he had not yet run into any proven cases.

That show confirmed for me the necessity of appearing on television and radio and giving print interviews. The public needed to be fully and fairly informed about the validity of psychic healing.

Nonetheless, an article that appeared a few months later had a nearly devastating effect on my career. In August 1975, a sensational tabloid reported on the HeLa cancer cell experiments in which I had participated at Lawrence Livermore Labs.

Word of the experiment had already circulated widely, and Judy, without naming names, had spoken about it at various conferences and lectures. The tabloid's reporter, knowing of my affiliation with Judy, had contacted me, and I had declined to comment on the experiment, but he was very persistent. "You're the one involved in the experiment, aren't you?" he demanded, and finally I said, "Yes, I'm involved, but I can't talk about it." He went on, reading me his information on the experiment. It was all accurate, but I just said again that I couldn't comment.

The article, when it appeared, was entirely accurate, but it was badly timed. People at Livermore were still sensitive about the publicity that had followed Uri Geller's work there. For a government-funded research institute affiliated with the Atomic Energy Commission and the University of California to receive publicity about its work with psychics was not good, as far as the director of publicity at the lab was concerned.

The man who had been responsible for getting me

and Geller into Livermore called me, frantic. He had been reprimanded by the public relations department and told not to do any more psychic research at the lab. That meant that I would not be given the opportunity to repeat the HeLa cancer cell experiment! He told me that even if I were to go to Livermore and levitate all the desks in the complex, the lab still would not want to have anything to do with psychic research. He was concerned about his job, and urged me to burn any papers given to me by the lab, especially my copy of an interdepartmental memo that confirmed the results of my experiments with the HeLa cancer cultures.

Of course, burning those papers was out of the question. Indeed, I only became more intent on repeating the experiment at another laboratory. How ironic it would seem latter when I found out that Livermore's major research effort at the time was the development of a neutron bomb.

My appearance on the network television show *Geraldo Rivera's Goodnight America* was yet another result of the article in the *Voice*. When I was contacted by Marty Berman, then the producer of the show, he told me he was impressed with what he'd read about my work—that I "demystified" psychic healing. He wanted to set up an interview for the following day, and I agreed enthusiastically.

I met Berman and five other staffers for my initial interview at ABC studios in Manhattan. Berman explained the plan for the show: Geraldo Rivera was going to expose a faith healer with questionable ethics, and he was looking for a "good" healer to represent the respected side of healing.

After establishing how I work and the kinds of cases I deal with, Berman asked if I could demonstrate my technique. Happy to comply, I turned to one of the production assistants and invited her to take a seat in front of me. As I began the laying on of hands, I felt very strong—I was really "cooking"—and I asked that someone throw a pen to the floor, because I felt I could do psychokinesis. Five pens hit the floor at once. I chose one, crouched on the carpet about six feet away, and made the necessary mental connection. The pen began to sweep across the rug toward me as everyone watched in astonishment.

As I fell exhausted on the carpet I heard soft whispering among the producers. Breathing deeply I pulled myself together, gave back the pen, and returned to my chair. Berman asked if it would be convenient for me to tape a show the following week.

My ego had played a large part in my performance of PK that day, and my body really suffered for it—I was violently ill afterward. It would be impossible for me to demonstrate this ability for the television audience. Berman noticed how drained I was after moving the pen, and he suggested that the network obtain a copy of some video tapes of the Faraday cage experiment I had participated in at Dakin Labs, and splice them into the show. I thought this was an excellent idea, but I was worried. The man who had asked me to burn the Livermore papers had worked with Dakin a great deal, and I knew Henry Dakin also took a dim view of publicity, so I doubted that Dakin would be of any help to the show. I was surprised to hear later that Dakin had indeed provided a tape of my electrostatic experiment.

A traditional medical doctor was asked to participate in the show to give it "balance." During his report on my work, Geraldo Rivera stated that six ABC staff members had seen me perform psychokinesis. When it was time for me to demonstrate my healing technique, Rivera selected his personal secretary, who had back pain, as my subject. Right on camera, as I worked on her, Rivera's secretary said she felt great relief. Rivera, uneasy, turned to the doctor for his opinion. The doctor's candid response was that from what he had just seen, psychic healing seemed to work. Rivera was speechless, but the doctor was impressed enough to refer a patient to me after the taping.

The show went wonderfully, with one major exception. The portion of the Faraday cage experiment that was aired showed the "control" portion of the experiment, in which I was not trying to produce an effect! How frustrated I was! Here was a long-awaited opportunity for a national audience to see me demonstrate PK under laboratory conditions, and the wrong segment of the tape was shown.

As my ego grew less attached to having publicity, I began to regard it as something of a nuisance, for interviews began to really crowd my schedule. As I got over the feeling that I had to prove my ability to other people I outgrew my interest in fame. Still, even with the problems and frustrations that have attended some of the publicity I've gotten, the media attention I've received has generally been a positive force. Many people have had their minds opened about psychic healing and some of the patients I have been able to help might never have come to me, were it not for the coverage I've received.

12.

Psychic Detective

Since childhood I have been fascinated with detective stories. I have spent many a night glued to the television set watching *Kojak* or *Police Story* reruns. Little did I know that this fascination would eventually lead me to a harrowing experience that had me literally in fear for my life.

From the time Yoko Ono told me about Peter Hurkos, a well-known Dutch psychic who works with the police in solving crimes and finding missing people, I was captivated by the idea of an alliance between psychics and the police. I felt that my own most important direction was healing, but I always wondered where the limits of my psychic abilities lay. When Helen Kruger, the writer, asked me to try psychometry, and I was able to tell her about the recently deceased woman whose keys I held, I became aware that my powers might not be limited to healing and psychokinesis.

One cold, cloudy evening in mid-1974, as I sat in

my folks' living room, which still served as my office, I received a call from a New Jersey attorney whom I'll call Peter Cory, who explained that his dilemma was not a health problem. His rebellious sixteen-year-old daughter Patty had been missing for three weeks, and though she had run away before, she had never been gone so long without contacting some member of the family. Knowing only too well the dangers that teenage runaways could encounter, Peter Cory asked me to try to help locate his child.

The thought of putting my psychometry to another test was intriguing, and I decided to give it a try. I listened to Mr. Cory's account of some of his daughter's escapades, but I felt I needed more information—perhaps a picture. I had heard that other psychics used pictures to help spark psychic flashes in similar cases.

A few days later I received an envelope containing the most recent picture Mr. Cory had of Patty. She was thin, with long, straight brown hair, and she looked much younger than sixteen. I read Mr. Cory's letter, which restated many of the facts he had told me over the phone, then studied the photo, trying to reach deep within myself for strong feelings, a mental picture, any connection at all. But I felt nothing.

Then I remembered that when I had done psychometry for Helen Kruger, holding the keys in my hand had definitely set something off inside of me. I contacted Mr. Cory again and asked him to send me a personal item that belonged to Patty.

In two days, I received a special delivery package containing a pair of earrings that Patty had often worn. Sitting at my desk, I gently placed the earrings in the center of my left palm, and immediately I felt a quickening of my pulse, so I closed my eyes and began to breathe slowly, calming myself so that any psychic impressions could flow freely. The earrings seemed to come alive in my hand, almost tingling.

With my right hand I absently picked up a pen and began to sketch on a piece of scrap paper. It was completely automatic—I felt that I wasn't in control of the pen. I concentrated intently on making a psychic connection with Patty Cory, and a picture began to form in my mind. Then I looked down at the white paper and saw the picture developing there, like a photographic image emerging on blank white paper in a darkroom.

I watched my hand—it didn't even seem to be part of my body anymore—and watched the light sketch lines turn into a building, a luncheonette on a street corner. The luncheonette had a large white sign, and I could clearly see vivid blue lettering advertising home-cooked meals and a friendly environment. My pen continued to move across the paper, and an L-shaped motel appeared just opposite the luncheonette. Tension began to build in my body as I felt myself getting closer to an answer. Then another large concrete building appeared. The signs I saw said it was a discotheque.

Pulling back, I realized that I'd drawn what appeared to be a section of a beach town or resort area. I had depicted a very wide expanse of beach—wider than any I could recall ever having seen—at the right side of the picture. Then the name "Wildwood" flashed, like a bolt of bright lightening, across my bewildered mind.

I immediately called Peter Cory, fumbling so with excitement and anxiety that I had to dial his phone number three times. He was stunned. Of course, he said, there was a town named Wildwood on the

Atlantic coast of New Jersey. This information fit in with the immense beach area that I had seen.

In response to a sudden, strong feeling, I instructed Mr. Cory to be in Wildwood on Thursday if he wanted to find his daughter. I didn't know why Thursday had come to mind but I felt it was very important. Mr. Cory said he'd be in Wildwood, accompanied by the local police, as soon as possible. Even though I didn't want to sound pushy, I felt compelled to repeat that he should be there no later than Thursday.

I must not have been emphatic enough, for Peter Cory called me the next weekend and told me that he and the police had gone to Wildwood, but not until Saturday. He hadn't found his daughter. Still, Mr. Cory described the beach town exactly as I had seen it—an L-shaped motel, a disco down the block, a luncheonette on the corner with blue lettering on the sign! Moreover, Mr. Cory had shown Patty's picture to many local people, and she had been identified by several employees of the motel and disco. But she had apparently left town on Friday!

I was frustrated, and I supposed I had heard the last of Peter Cory. But about three weeks later he phoned and told me my information had been most helpful after all. He and the police had followed up the leads they'd uncovered in Wildwood and had finally found Patty, in good health, in another nearby resort area. This news was enormously encouraging, and I was learning more and more to retain confidence in my intuitions.

Two years later the opportunity to play psychic detective and work with the New York City Police Department presented itself. In 1976, I got a call from Detective John McGrath of the Brooklyn Robbery Squad, who had been referred by Judy Skutch. Judy had mentioned to him my fascination with psychic detective work, and he wanted to know if I would like to tackle a robbery case that had the police baffled. I was indeed eager to see if I could help, and I invited the detective to my office.

Later that day Rochelle escorted two plainclothes detectives into my office. Detective McGrath was a tall, friendly man in his late thirties, with red hair and a thick mustache. He wore a sport jacket, an open-necked shirt, and tan slacks. He introduced his companion, whose cool attitude felt like a sudden chill wind in the still room, but I ignored it as McGrath described his own background. The holder of a master's degree in forensic psychology, McGrath had originated a hypnosis program in the police department, taught hypnosis courses at the police academy, and was clearly an innovative thinker in criminal work. He was fascinated by psychics and enthusiastic about using them to help solve difficult cases. He had worked with two psychics in the past, and their aid had been valuable.

Then McGrath described the case at hand. Only a few days before, $500,000 had been stolen from a Hassidic rabbi and his two daughters, who had just withdrawn the money from a Manhattan bank. The police had no good leads.

I started to relax in my chair, asking the detectives to take notes on anything I said, for excitement was welling up as I suddenly began to see pictures and words forming in my mind. This experience was different from earlier ones—the pictures were coming so fast. I felt a thick lump developing in my chest as mental images flashed like neon signs.

"The robbers live in Brooklyn, maybe in the Bensonhurst or Bay Ridge sections," I told the policemen, suddenly feeling great confidence in this information. "One of the perpetrators," I added, self-consciously using what I supposed was police language, "lives on Eighty-sixth Street and Twenty-first Avenue. The money was dropped off near there, around Eighty-sixth Street and Bay Parkway."

I took a breather. The second detective was looking at me skeptically, but Detective McGrath was enthralled, sitting on the edge of his seat and hanging on everything I said. Then another word flashed before me: *Joey.* I was sure that one of the robbers was named Joey.

The second detective checked his list of possible suspects, smirking as he told me that there was no Joey there. But he added the name to the list. Then I was exhausted. All the information I had related had seemed to flow easily enough, but now I was drained of strength and energy.

After the detectives left, promising to call if there was any progress in the case, Rochelle came into my office, eager to know the details of their visit. When I recounted what had happened, I wondered momentarily if she would believe that I had perceived information about the case. But her only concern was for my safety—what if "Joey" found out that I had put the finger on him? I had to grin, for Rochelle hadn't doubted the accuracy of my information for a moment.

Two weeks after my meeting with Detective McGrath he called in with great excitement to tell me that the leads I had given him had proven to be exactly right! The stolen money had been dropped off near an ice-cream parlor on Eighty-sixth Street and Bay Parkway in the Bensonhurst-Bay Ridge section of Brooklyn. The police had retrieved some of the money, though part of it was missing. Two suspects had been identified. One of them resided near the ice-cream parlor, at Eighty-sixth Street and Twenty-first Avenue. But he was dead; his body had been found in New Jersey, lying near a car belonging to the second suspect. The dead man's name: Joey.

I was awed by what McGrath told me. These curious new-found abilities of mine were proving to be on the mark much more consistently than I'd ever hoped.

Three months later Detective McGrath called again. The police had just apprehended the second robbery suspect at Kennedy Airport. He was carrying $144,000 of the stolen money. McGrath told me emphatically that he was very impressed by the accuracy of my information, which he said went "beyond luck." Though he had consulted psychics in the past, he said, none had ever been quite as accurate as I. But, he added, police don't really know how to utilize the information they get from psychics who are working with them. "You're dealing in a time and space frame that the police department doesn't know how to deal with," he told me. "It will take us time to catch up to your abilities and use your information more accurately."

Several months later Detective McGrath contacted me again and asked if I would like to get involved in a puzzling year-old homicide case. The police department had already authorized my immediate involvement. A mixture of vanity and curiosity prompted my instant agreement.

A week later Detective McGrath came to my office with Detective John O'Flaherty, a veteran of the homicide squad, who told me he'd never worked with a psychic before, but that he'd been extremely impressed with my work on the robbery. O'Flaherty related the facts of the homicide case: A year earlier, a Brooklyn man in his early forties had started his day as usual, breakfasting with his wife and two children and kissing them good-bye before leaving for work. He was never seen again. The police had discovered his beat-up cream-colored Ford Fairlane parked down by the docks in south Brooklyn. A tremendous amount of the man's blood and brain matter were spattered over the front seat and around the car, and his tortoiseshell-framed glasses, stained with blood and missing one lens, lay inside. But there was no body. After a year the police still hadn't found the corpse and didn't have the vaguest idea who had killed the man.

McGrath pulled out an envelope containing two photographs—one of the murdered man and another of his car—and the man's bloodied eyeglasses. I held the glasses in my hand while I studied the pictures, but I didn't feel any sensations from them. What I did feel was the desire to see, perhaps even sit in, the dead man's car, and I told the detectives so.

My office wasn't far from the victim's home, so Detective McGrath suggested we go there. The man's widow worked near her home and I could get a picture of his neighborhood before sitting in the car.

As we left my office the detectives pointed to a taxi parked across the street—their unmarked car. As I slid into the back seat I couldn't help but think, "Move over, Kojak!"

Our first stop was Bensonhurst, Brooklyn, where the murdered man had lived peacefully with his family. As we slowly cruised the residential street O'Flaherty pointed out the murdered man's house

—one of the row of seven or eight similar houses, red brick with five steps leading to the front door. McGrath discreetly pointed to a huge, rough-looking man in a long leather jacket who stood talking to a shorter, slighter man on the street near the victim's house. The big man was a suspect in the case, McGrath explained, for he'd been reported to have exchanged threats with the victim after a domestic dispute. He was known to get into fights frequently, and he had a criminal record. Looking at the two men on the street, I felt certain that if I could somehow look into the suspect's eyes, I could tell if he was involved in the case.

O'Flaherty turned the corner, stopped the cab, and asked if I had gotten any special feelings about the suspect as we passed him. I told him about my need to look the man in the eyes. Eager to assist me, O'Flaherty suggested that he and McGrath cover me while I approached the man and asked for directions.

I could hardly believe what I had gotten myself into, but I watched as the cops took their positions. McGrath remained on the corner near where we had parked and O'Flaherty jogged briskly around the block to end up at the far corner, beyond the spot where the two men stood talking. After getting a slight nod from McGrath, I slowly made my way down the lengthy street. I tried to appear casual, but I did glance over my shoulder once, to see McGrath lounging against a building, apparently reading a newspaper. Then I looked toward the corner ahead of me, but at first I couldn't see O'Flaherty. I felt a quiver in the pit of my stomach. What the hell was I doing here? I felt some relief when I finally saw O'Flaherty watching me discreetly, his head barely visible. But I was still scared.

I finally drew near the two men, and when the man in question noticed me I quickly walked up to him and asked for directions, making sure to look directly into his eyes, which were dark brown and piercing.

Immediately I felt great relief, for I sensed that this was an innocent man, certainly not a murderer. When our eyes met my fears dissipated, and I knew I was in no danger. I thanked the man for his help and turned and walked back up the block. My heart was still pounding so hard it almost hurt, but I concentrated on moving slowly and naturally. When I turned the corner, both detectives were waiting for me, eager to hear my impression of the suspect. I told them that my strong intuition was that the man was not the murderer.

Back in the taxi I felt uncomfortable and drained, but I ignored my feelings and asked the detectives what our next stop was. They drove down another street in the neighborhood and pointed out a dry-cleaning store where a pale and drawn-looking middle-aged woman sat bent over a sewing machine near the window. She was the dead man's widow. McGrath led me into the store and introduced me to the woman. I chatted casually with her for a few moments, but I didn't get any feelings about the case.

From the store we drove toward the Brooklyn docks, where the man's car had originally been found. Privately I questioned whether I could "feel" anything from the supposed scene of the murder, since it had happened over a year before. Moreover, the car might have been transported from another location after the murder was committed.

We parked in the spot where the car had been found, and I closed my eyes, trying to clear my mind of thoughts and fears. It wasn't easy, for I was growing very tired. Again, I felt nothing, so I suggested once more that I actually sit in the car in which the murder had taken place. The car was being held at an old police compound in a housing development in Brooklyn, and we decided to make that our final stop for the day. I was glad, for I was exhausted.

We found the Ford parked in the rear of the old police compound. Looking inside I saw the dark blood stains and what I imagined to be bits of human tissue. McGrath got a big white sheet, covered the seat with it, and, cracking a joke to break the tension, invited me to sit inside. Then he and O'Flaherty went to wait for me in the taxi.

As I lowered my body onto the front seat I felt the cool autumn wind raise goose bumps on my arms. There was a terrible odor in the car, and it made me nauseous. Almost without realizing it, I began to hyperventilate. The pain in my lungs was strong and the nausea kept rising, while I fought to hold it down.

Then a picture—a clear picture in vivid color —blazed in my mind. I saw a short, stocky man with a pasty, pock-marked complexion, curly black hair and a wide hooked nose. I felt my pulse race as I focused on his long, white apron, the kind worn by a butcher. It was covered with dark red stains. My mind ached and I was very frightened.

As though I were watching a slide show, a new image flashed into place. It was a gun—a silver .38 with a mother-of-pearl handle. Part of the butt was broken off.

Then, quite abruptly, I knew that I had received all the impressions I was going to while sitting in the car. I was glad to be finished. I got out, leaving the sheet covering most of the mess, and walked to the cab where O'Flaherty and McGrath waited.

I described the images I had received, and when I was finished O'Flaherty's face was drained of all color. Wordlessly he removed a black-and-white Polaroid picture from his shirt pocket and handed it to me. There was the same man I had "seen"—dark curly hair, hooked nose, pitted complexion and bloodied apron. He was the dead man's brother-in-law, McGrath told me excitedly. He had recently become a suspect because he had expressed excessive concern over his relative's death.

As McGrath drove me to Rochelle's parents' house to meet Rochelle, he told me that for some time the police had suspected that the murder was somehow connected with a meat-packing conspiracy. He and O'Flaherty decided they'd like me to go with them to a meat-packing plant where I might obtain further clues as to the location of the dead man's body or the reason for his murder. McGrath and O'Flaherty grew more and more excited as they discussed the implications of the images I'd described, but I barely had the strength to stretch out my legs and lean my head back.

We pulled up to my in-laws' house, and I shook hands with the two policemen as they thanked me for my help. I watched the taxi pull away, then turned and walked up the steps, feeling like an old man. I told Rochelle everything that had transpired since morning, and she grew concerned for my health, for the day's adventures had taken a lot out of me. I admitted to her that the police wanted me to continue working on the case. Rochelle was against my going on, though she left the final decision up to me, and I found myself completely in agreement.

The psychometry had affected my body very

negatively. I felt so depleted, so weak and nauseous, that I didn't think I could continue. I could have healed fifty people a day for three days straight and not have been as drained. I also felt that if I continued working on the murder case I might be placing myself, and perhaps my family, in danger. As hard as I tried, I couldn't visualize my going any further with the investigation. For me, the case was closed.

Long after I'd withdrawn from the case, I contacted McGrath to find out how it had been resolved, and he told me that the case had been dropped shortly after I'd pulled out. Because the corpse had never been found, technically there had been no homicide.

I like excitement and I am always curious to see what the limits of my ability are. I gained a great deal of valuable knowledge about myself and my psychic potential by working with the police, and I was encouraged once again to trust my intuitions. But even though playing psychic detective had been a great adventure for a while, its rewards just couldn't compare with those of a healing experience.

13.

Mending Bodies, Mending Minds

Only a few days after I'd worked with McGrath and O'Flaherty my priorities were quickly and clearly reaffirmed when three-and-a-half-month-old Jennifer Paul was brought to my office by her parents. Jennifer had been born with severe nerve damage and an inner ear malfunction, and had been pronounced "severely to profoundly deaf" by an otolaryngologist at Long Island Jewish Hospital and by the director of the Lexington School for the Deaf. Though an infant, she was already enrolled at the Lexington School, but the only help they held out was eventual speech therapy and a hearing aid. Jennifer's condition was considered incurable.

I asked the young mother to sit on my recliner with Jennifer on her knee. As I focused my energy on the baby's head and ears, Irwin Paul said that since his daughter's hearing had just been tested at her school—the test had revealed a seventy percent hearing loss—any improvement would be easy to gauge.

A few weeks later Mr. Paul called with wonderful news. Since my session with Jennifer, she had seemed to be more responsive to his voice and to other sounds, and he had just taken her for retesting. Mr. Paul started to choke up as he told me that the new test indicated a hearing loss of only thirty percent. The Lexington School personnel had been unable to explain this sudden and unexpected improvement. They had simply removed Jennifer's hearing aid and told her astonished father that she could no longer be enrolled in a program for the hearing impaired.

Mr. Paul, a high-school guidance counselor and former science teacher, was what I call an open-minded skeptic. He respected scientific principles, but was willing to look beyond their boundaries. He told me quite candidly that he didn't know whether to attribute Jennifer's improvement to my treatment or to a remarkable coincidence. All he knew for sure was that right after he had brought Jennifer to see me she had begun to hear, and the doctors didn't know why.

The last time I heard from Jennifer's parents, her hearing had improved until no deficiency at all could be detected. I had never worked on an infant before, and I was moved by the idea of restoring the priceless gift of hearing to a tiny baby. But the case of Jennifer Paul was also important in my search for validation of my healing ability. Jennifer had been declared clinically deaf before I treated her, and now she could hear. Let someone try to take this cure and attribute it to "suggestion"!

It was a great joy to me to know that little Jennifer, expected to grow up deaf, would instead have a normal life, filled with the richness of sound that most of us take for granted. Her life had been changed at its very outset. The healing of some of my more mature patients has given me another sort of joy, when the end of illness has enabled them to return to a way of life that had once been full but that seemed in danger of being taken from them forever. Certainly a disease need not be truly "life-threatening," like cancer, to threaten the way of life a person thinks most worth living.

Ballet dancer Jeffrey Baker traveled from Ontario, Canada, for treatment. He was totally debilitated by colitis, an intestinal problem causing continuous diarrhea and severe abdominal pain. He had lost twenty-five pounds in two months, and although he was under a doctor's care, his medication wasn't working and the pounds were continuing to drop from his already thin body. To compound his dismay, the prolonged physical trauma of his career had left his knees constantly sore, making it difficult for him to dance. He was terribly depressed.

Since colitis is believed to be a stress-related problem, I focused a large part of my treatments on relaxing Jeffrey's body. After the first session he called to let me know that he felt much stronger. By the third session he came bouncing into my office. He had gained seven pounds in six days, the gnawing cramps he'd felt for two months had subsided, and his knees were less sore. In another two days, Jeffrey gained a total of almost ten pounds, and the cramps, the debilitating diarrhea, and the knee soreness were all completely gone.

Jeffrey was close to me in age, and I was not far from the days when I'd aspired to a career in music. When, in a relatively short time, Jeffrey was able to return to dancing, I felt a very special gratification.

Another artist whose career was endangered was Leonard Rose, a virtuoso cellist, formerly a member of the New York Philharmonic, and part of the acclaimed Istomin-Stern-Rose Trio. Fifty-eight and a handsome man, Rose faced a grave problem—he had developed a severe weakness in his left hand caused by a pinched nerve in the back of his neck. In addition, he had tennis elbow—in this case really cellist's elbow—and the muscles in his arm were beginning to atrophy. Pain and weakness made it almost impossible for him to perform, and the threat to his career had left his morale at a low ebb.

During five weeks of treatment, Rose improved steadily, and soon after, he left on a long-awaited worldwide concert tour. When he returned he called to let me know that he had experienced no problems with his arm. Later Rochelle and I happened to see Leonard performing on television, and we were touched and delighted.

Like the case of Jennifer Paul, the case of a man I'll call Robert Lewin enabled me to secure at least limited validation from the world of traditional medicine. Lewin, a thirty-eight-year-old real estate agent, had visited his ophthalmologist a week before his first session with me. His visual acuity had been measured at 20/30—near normal—in his right eye, and at 6/200—severely nearsighted—in his left eye. In the center back of his left eye, the doctor had discovered an old scar with a small hemorrhage above it that was obstructing Robert's vision.

Since doctors at Montefiore Hospital had not encouraged Robert about the possibility of halting the degeneration of his eyesight, he wanted to give my treatment a chance. During our sessions I concentrated on trying to stop the hemorrhage in Robert's eye. Nine days after our first session Robert returned to his doctor and was told that the vision in his left eye had improved to 20/200, though there had been no change in the hemorrhage in the rear of the eye. Still, Robert and I were encouraged by that first improvement and Robert began coming to me regularly. As time passed he reported that his vision had cleared noticeably. After eight months he returned to his ophthalmologist.

This time Robert's "good" right eye had improved a bit, to 20/25. The vision in his left eye had increased dramatically, to 20/50, and the hemorrhage in the back of the eye was gone. At my request Robert asked his doctor to send me a letter confiming these changes. The physician refused to send the letter to me, but he did address a written report to Robert. His letter recorded the changes in Robert's vision and noted, "I mentioned to you that it was possible that the hemorrhage would clear by itself and that you would have some resulting improvement in visual acuity, though this was not likely."

Following an automobile accident nine years before I met him, Sean Bart, as I'll call him, had undergone repeated operations, including plastic surgery, on an ankle wound. For the past three years the wound had simply refused to heal. Despite every available therapy it remained open and gaping. But after our second session together Sean's doctor noticed that the character of the wound had suddenly changed. Within a few weeks of our fourth and final session the wound was closed.

Marilyn Englese had been living in the personal hell of severe depression for seven years when she came to see me. The attractive mother of two girls, she was taking heavy doses of antidepressant medicine, but wanted to find a natural way to help herself. She had tried transcendental meditation for three years, had been under a psychiatrist's care for a year, and had undergone megavitamin therapy at the Nassau Mental Health Center for two years. Still, as she later recalled in a letter, she felt that she was "living in darkness, never again to see the light."

During our first session I concentrated on Marilyn's mid-forehead, neck, and shoulders. I felt I wanted to "cool down" her central nervous system and lower her level of stress and tension. Marilyn responded very slowly at first, but I felt certain that I could help her, so when she suggested coming to see me more than once a week I agreed. I thought that if I had more opportunities to transfer energy into her body, her depression might begin to lift more quickly.

Soon Marilyn began to improve. Within the next few months she reported that sometimes she woke up feeling happy just to be alive. At first those instances were scattered, but over time they began to occur more consistently. Finally Marilyn asked if I thought she could give up the medication she had needed for years. She had tried several times in the past to stop taking her antidepressant pills, but she'd always become so nervous and upset that she had been forced to resume taking them. I told her that I believed that my clients should continue all medications and therapies outlined by their medical doctors, unless the recommendations were changed by the doctors themselves.

Marilyn understood my position, so she approached her doctor, explained that she'd been feeling much better for the last several months, and asked him to stop her medication. Her physician studied her, noted that all signs of her depression were gone, and agreed.

A year later she still hadn't taken another antidepressant. I know, because that's when she came to work for Rochelle and me as our secretary. Not only was she terrific in the office, but she was a great representative for my work. Whenever someone asked, "Does he *really* work?" Marilyn was ready to jump in with her personal testimony.

Marilyn's case was of great interest to me, for she was the first client whom I treated for a condition that was mental or emotional, rather than strictly physical. Still, I've discovered that illness always produces a mental effect, as well as physical manifestations. When people come to me they are usually very depressed, though they don't have clinical depression like Marilyn's. It's very gratifying to see people's lives changed by coming into my office. One of the special rewards of my work is to see people go back to work—and play—with both their health and happiness restored.

14.

The Foundation for Psychic-Energetic Research

From the time of my first, disappointing research experience in California, Rochelle and I constantly discussed the state of current thinking on psychic phenomena and the conflicting political forces within the world of parapsychology. Even after my more gratifying second research trip, we spent a great deal of time trying to think of a way to set up an experimental situation closer to home, where I could be tested on a regular, ongoing basis. We had been fascinated by the scientific procedures utilized during my California trips, and wondered whether we could get more directly involved in testing ourselves. The idea of setting up our own parapsychology research foundation began to occupy our minds more and more.

Our main goal was to find out the source of the "energy" with which I heal and to explore how its benefits could be applied to mankind. We had a dream that if, for example, it were determined that I heal by affecting force fields, it might be possible to build a machine that could similarly alter force fields and thus heal. If what I'm all about could be determined, then it might be possible to synthesize my healing energy.

Rochelle and I had become involved with a number of parapsychology researchers and sympathizers, and we thought it would be useful to bring all their heads together at regular meetings. We began to envision our foundation as a sort of East Coast think tank. We also saw it as a vehicle for finding other people with abilities like mine. People contact us constantly saying, "I think I have psychic ability. What should I do?" We thought our foundation could help such people explore their psychic potential.

Another goal was to help healing research stand on its own, independent of politics and selfish maneuvering. Our foundation might help parapsychology research in general evolve from its still embryonic state. And if we could publicize the results of our testing, we might achieve acceptance and respectability for the nonreligious laying on of hands as a supplemental nonpharmacological therapy, used in conjunction with traditional Western medicine.

Our first step was to propose the idea to Judy. She responded with immediate enthusiasm, for she wanted me to have my own look at the researcher's side of research. She suggested we meet with her and Paul Silverman, our lawyer, to discuss the details. In subsequent meetings we decided to dub our foundation the Foundation for Psychic-Energetic Research. We established a board of directors that included doctors and other people interested in parapsychology, and Paul began putting together the papers necessary to apply to the Internal Revenue Service for tax-exempt status, which would make it easier for us to raise money for our projects.

Despite my success in the labs and the written testimonies of many clients whom I had helped, the IRS turned down our request for tax-exempt status. When Paul protested the decision, they responded by setting a date for a meeting.

On the appointed day Paul and I caught the Eastern shuttle to Washington, D.C. In spite of myself, the idea of meeting with the IRS for any purpose filled me with anxiety, and I was in a bad mood. When Paul said to me, "Dean, I think it would be best if you allow me to deal with the IRS people; I speak their language," I exploded.

"You speak their language! Then why are we on the way to Washington to fight their ruling?" I demanded. "If you can't get your points across this time, you'd better believe I'll say what I have to! Maybe if they'd understood our purpose the first time, they would have granted the tax-exempt status!"

Immediately I felt ashamed of myself. Like me, Paul had a lot at stake in this meeting. This was his first attempt at establishing a public research foundation. Recalling the care that had gone into the well-organized papers Paul had submitted to the IRS, I apologized for my outburst.

When we got to Washington we caught a cab to the Internal Revenue Service headquarters at 1111 Constitution Avenue, a massive and imposing stone office building. Inside, in front of Room 303, we stopped to compose ourselves. Then I turned the knob on the door.

Two men sat inside at a long walnut conference table.

"Mr. Daniels?" I inquired.

The taller and older man stood and extended his hand. Steven Daniels, as I'll call him, was lean, in his mid-fifties, conservatively dressed. He had clear, appraising eyes. His assistant, whom I'll call Robert Wexler, a stocky man in his early forties, also rose to shake hands. Then we all sat down.

Paul opened his briefcase, removed two four-inch-thick packages and handed one to each of them, explaining that they contained selected documentation of my years of work in psychic healing and research. Included were medical and scientific reports, personal testimonials from clients, and articles from national magazines ranging from *Scientific American* to *Cosmopolitan.*

Mr. Daniels opened his folder and began to read, moving papers from one side to the other and back again, as if to check one report against another. I glanced at Paul to see who would make the first move. Minutes passed in silence, and I grew edgy. Finally Mr. Daniels raised his eyes, looked at me and said, "Tell us a bit more about your work."

Immediately Paul jumped in.

"Approximately four years ago, Mr. Daniels, Mr. Kraft discovered something 'different' about himself. He felt a curious energy emanating from his body, an energy over which he seems to have definite control. He himself is not sure what this energy is. There are many forms of energy all around us, invisible but present. For example, we can't see radio or television waves, but we know they exist. Mr. Kraft feels that through deep mental concentration he is able to absorb energy from his environment, and that then, by the 'laying on of hands,' he can channel that energy to an ill person, usually someone who has exhausted all available medical avenues. For about three years Mr. Kraft has worked with many patients referred to him by medical doctors. These doctors have reported that malignant tumors have shrunk, paralysis has disappeared, arthritics have experienced less pain and much improved movement.''

Paul paused to let his words sink in, then turned to the documents in front of him.

"I'd like to bring your attention to the yellow folder you have, in which you will find numerous letters and testimonials from physicians who, without being able to offer any explanations for the unexpected improvements in their patients, nevertheless are prepared to attest to their veracity. You'll see that against high odds and poor prognoses, many of these people have been helped by Mr. Kraft's healing energy.''

I listened as Paul presented our arguments in his carefully modulated voice. He spoke of the tradition of spiritual and faith healing going back to the time of Christ, adding quickly that I didn't claim any religious element in my psychic healing. Paul and I had discussed all this information in detail many times.

When Mr. Daniels asked about the experiments I had done at the Lawrence Livermore Labs, Paul told them that I had been able to break apart a percentage of the cells in a test tube of very aggressive cancer cells, and that the alteration of the cells had been documented by microscopic analysis after the session. He explained that too little research had been done for anyone to reach any final conclusions, but that most researchers felt that further tests could be very helpful, and that I was eager to submit myself to the widest possible range of testing to prove that my healing energy really exists and works, and to find out, if possible, what it is.

Paul then settled back in his chair and signaled me with a wink.

I jumped from my seat, reminding myself to speak slowly, for I feared I would babble in my anxiety.

"Gentlemen, one of our foundation's main purposes is to investigate and explore the phenomenon of 'mind-energy' and to report on it in a scientific and unbiased manner. We are trying to advance 'psychic-energetic' or 'mind-energy' therapy into a science. We hope to establish a research foundation equipped with sophisticated, sensitive equipment similar to that on which I have been tested in other institutions.

"I am convinced that there are many people who possess the same 'energy' I do, perhaps in varying degrees. The Foundation for Psychic-Energetic Research wants to seek out these individuals and test them. If any significant effects are obtained in our tests, we will then try to train these people to utilize their 'energy' to help mankind."

Mr. Daniels asked me to provide details on a few of the experiments in which I had been involved and I described the results of the tests involving plant growth and the Faraday cage at Dakin Labs, the startling outcome of my attempt to lower the rat's blood pressure, and the various EEG tests I had undergone. I tried to emphasize once again that the aim of our foundation was to explore a very promising area for scientific research, one that might offer an enormous benefit to humanity.

After my lengthy statement I dropped back into my seat. Paul was gently kicking me under the table and when I turned to him, he grinned.

"I must say this case is unique," Mr. Daniels told us. "Psychic healing—is there a way you can describe for us what is involved in a 'treatment' with this 'energy'?"

"Why don't I give you a demonstration?" I said. I got up, took off my jacket, rolled up my sleeves and walked over to the chair in which Mr. Daniels was sitting. Standing behind him, I closed my eyes and began to breathe deeply and slowly. Quickly passing into a relaxed state, I placed my right hand on Mr. Daniels' tense forehead and my left on his back.

Lifting his head sharply Mr. Daniels twisted around in his chair to look at me.

"It's unbelievable! It feels as though you're plugged into an electric socket or something!"

He gestured excitedly toward his assistant. "Him, show him!"

I moved behind Mr. Wexler, who had been quietly observing. His body jerked slightly when I touched his back and neck. After a few minutes, I returned to my seat next to Paul, and the two IRS representatives regarded each other wide-eyed and flushed, then spoke quietly between themselves.

Finally Mr. Wexler leaned back in his seat and Mr. Daniels began to address us, speaking now with a tone of respectful interest.

"To grant this type of research organization tax-exempt status would be to establish a precedent. Public foundations in this area, excluding the religious category, of course, are almost nonexistent. Parapsychology is an area in which, up to this time, it has been extremely difficult to evaluate achievements in terms of scientific measurement.

"However, with what we see here today—"

"And feel—" interjected Mr. Wexler.

"With what we see and feel, I believe that the original problem with granting the Foundation for Psychic-Energetic Research total tax-exemption must have been one of communication between your representatives and ourselves. I'm very glad to have had a chanee to meet you, Mr. Kraft. I'm sure we can see our way clear to grant you tax-exempt status."

I could barely contain my delight as Paul and I gathered up our papers, thanked Mr. Daniels and Mr. Wexler and left. As soon as we got outside, I erupted. "We did it!" I yelled, giving Paul a huge bear hug and almost lifting him off the sidewalk.

I was excited that we had opened the minds of the IRS representatives. At the time the IRS gave our foundation tax-exempt status, I was the first living psychic healer to establish such a foundation. A similar organization had been founded in Edgar Cayce's name, but not until after his death. I knew that the IRS ruling couldn't promise acceptance of my work. But I felt a heady sense of accomplishment, because an important branch of our government had, in its own way, acknowledged that psychic healing and psychic energy were legitimate areas for research.

In the months after the IRS decision the Foundation for Psychic-Energetic Research became involved in its first experiments. In the first, conducted at a major Southern cancer center with Rochelle and me acting as the experimenters, ten healers tried to duplicate the effect I had produced on the HeLa cancer cells, but none succeeded. In the second, at an East Coast university, I treated nine people with chronic ailments who had failed to find relief through traditional medical routes or biofeedback training. All but one subject experienced at least a degree of improvement after I worked with them.

But these experiments were just baby steps for our foundation. The real work lies ahead, right now represented only by a number of experimental designs. I want to continue to search for other people with abilities like mine. And the ultimate goal remains: to find out what my energy is, to quantify it, and then to try to synthesize it. Research into healing and psychic energy is an open territory for any pioneers willing and able to explore it, and that's how we see ourselves: as explorers in a new and tremendously exciting field.

15.

Victory in the Lab: Destroying HeLa

In July 1977, I was finally given the opportunity to try to replicate the HeLa cancer cell experiment performed at Lawrence Livermore Laboratories. Dr. John M. Kmetz, director of research at the Science Unlimited Research Foundation (SURF) in San Antonio, Texas, was not only willing to conduct the experiment, but had promised to stand by the results publicly.

SURF is a highly technical, privately funded laboratory that has been delving into the paranormal since 1972. It was at the suggestion of one of SURF's trustees who was familiar with my work that Dr. Kmetz had contacted me.

Dr. Kmetz, a physiologist and a former professor at Penn State University, had done extensive work in parapsychology, and was a rigorous and skeptical researcher. Shortly before my trip to San Antonio he had published a paper in *The Humanist* challenging the work of Cleve Backster, who had claimed to demonstrate that plants are affected by human thoughts. Two years of strictly controlled experiments had not supported Backster's findings. I found Kmetz friendly but formal as he guided Rochelle and me through the maze of offices and laboratories at SURF's headquarters.

I was still somewhat annoyed that my planned trip to Livermore to repeat the HeLa experiment had been scuttled because of the blowup over publicity. This experiment was important for so many reasons—it would give me credibility; it would help prove that psychic healing works clinically; and it would signify an attempt to find an alternate, non-toxic means of killing cancer cells.

To think that I had affected the cells in my first trial at Livermore was mind-blowing. To know that no other healer had been able to duplicate the feat was nerve-racking. Would I be able to do it again? If I achieved the same effects as I had at Livermore—dislodging twice as many free-floating cells from the experimental culture as floated in the control culture—the experiment would be a success.

Dr. Kmetz had been working on a new experimental design for a couple of months before my arrival, and he had greatly improved on Livermore's design. Fortunately the Livermore papers, which I never did burn, were a great help. In order to properly replicate the Livermore experiment the new procedure had to utilize the same materials—the same type of culture, flasks, and liquid medium—as the original. The changes Kmetz made were aimed at establishing tighter controls. Before I even got to the lab he had conducted test runs, with other subjects claiming healing ability and with volunteers from the University of Texas, where he taught physiology, working on the cells. None of them had been able to change the state of the HeLa cells to any significant degree.

When the HeLa cell culture grows in a flask, the cells adhere, like glue to the glass, in a single layer that eventually covers the bottom of the container. HeLa cells adhere so firmly that Kmetz had found that when he threw flasks against a wall, shook them vigorously, even put them on a vibrating machine, only a very few mature cells floated to the top of the medium.

The first day I visited the SURF, Kmetz and his young assistant, Jim, led me into a dimly lit nine-foot-by-twelve-foot room with a door like a bank vault. Jim was very curious about my healing technique, and rather than try to explain, I decided to demonstrate. I had Jim sit in a black vinyl chair in the center of the small room, while Kmetz sat on a couch by the wall to observe. Standing behind Jim, with my left hand on his forehead and my right on the back of his neck, I closed my eyes and began to concentrate on relaxing his general nervous system. Despite my anxiety over the cancer experiment, when I moved my hands to Jim's shoulders, I felt great. I had a sudden, strong urge to attempt psychokinesis, but I dismissed the idea, feeling that it might drain me and prevent me from performing optimally during the experiments. Still, the energy was building fast, and I began to feel the need to release it. I had experienced the same sensation—almost a *need* to do PK—in the past, and when I'd given into it, I hadn't felt too sick or drained.

Following my intuition, I moved from behind Jim's chair to the small area in front of both researchers, and asked Kmetz for his pen. He handed it to me, and I immediately let it drop to the floor a few feet in front of me. The connection between my mind and the pen was very strong. I began to lean back, with my hands extended toward my target, and the pen moved steadily toward me. After a few seconds, I fell to the floor retching, my heart pounding. It was all I could do to ask the stunned Kmetz to get Rochelle.

After I recovered I really wondered whether I had enough strength to resume the work schedule for the day. But Dr. Kmetz was most understanding. He suggested I go back to the hotel and rest for a few hours—maybe take a swim—and return to the lab later in the day.

As Rochelle and I relaxed in the hotel pool, I was glad that I had been able to perform PK for the two scientists. But moving the pen could no way compare with affecting cancer cells. As soon as I could I went back to the lab, ready to undertake my real task.

As we sat in the same shielded room where I'd performed PK, Dr. Kmetz explained that he wanted me to do the same thing I'd done at Livermore—cause an increase in the number of free-floating—dead—cancer cells. The number of floating cells would be measured by a hemacytometer before and after the experiment. Kmetz also wanted to use microscopic examination to see what happened inside the cells I worked on.

Dr. Kmetz wanted Jim, who didn't claim any healing ability, to act as one control, "healing" a vial of cells by copying my actions. A second control vial would not be treated at all. The three vials were selected randomly, and Jim and I went to work.

As I held the clear flask, I was determined to overcome my lingering fatigue and affect the cells. Concentrating on the picture I'd formed in my mind of the cells, I directed my thoughts to the flask and visualized a disturbance in the cell fields and the cells blowing up. I was aware of Jim mimicking my motions—when I held both hands over my flask he did the same, and when I began breathing deeply I heard him start to take deep breaths.

After twenty minutes I knew that I'd affected the cells. I sensed a definite interaction, almost a magnetic pull, between my hands and the flask. Before he tested the contents of the flask, I told Dr. Kmetz my feeling. Sure enough, when he tested the cell culture I had treated he found that I had significantly increased the number of cells floating on top of the medium. After the flask was swirled gently to evenly distribute the free-floating cells, the hemacytometer indicated an increase from one to two floaters per field to six to seven per field—a field being an arbitrary segment of the area visible under the microscope. Dr. Kmetz then tested the control flask Jim had worked with and found no change from the original number of floating cells. The untreated control flask was also unchanged.

I was very excited because at Livermore I'd only been able to double the number of floating cells in the experimental flask. It was nearly time for the lab to close; our tests would resume in the morning. I was sure I could do even better then, for I felt the PK earlier in the day had drained me after all.

The next day we conducted a similar experiment, but this time I worked on one flask of cells for three twenty-minute periods. Kmetz wanted to see if I could continue to increase the number of free-floating cells with successive treatments. The cells were counted after each twenty-minute interval, after

I reported whether I felt I had affected the cells. With the first two trials I felt I hadn't made a connection, and sure enough the hemacytometer showed no significant change in the number of floating cells. Dr. Kmetz was obviously amazed that I could tell whether I had affected the cells. He'd never before tested anyone who could tell how he or she had done before the results were analyzed.

Before going on to my third trial Dr. Kmetz conducted a test to check again whether vigorous shaking could cause any more cells to break loose from the cell layer on the bottom of the flask. It had no effect.

Then I began my final session with the flask of cancer cells. I knew I would have to put everything I had into this final twenty minutes, and it was by far the most difficult session I encountered. While I worked I could feel a virtual tug-of-war going on between my hands and the cells' powerful adhesive ability. Then I felt the field give way. I felt I'd broken through, and I was certain that something important would come of this trial.

Anxiously I waited for Dr. Kmetz to evaluate the results, hoping he would confirm what I had already described to him as a struggle. Dr. Kmetz returned from testing the culture looking almost befuddled. He told us he'd never witnessed such a remarkable scene under a microscope. Not only had I substantially increased the number of floating cells, but the cells looked as though someone had put a tiny hand grenade into each one—the whole culture had just blown apart! The number of floating cells had increased twenty times.

Dr. Kmetz showed me his work sheets and let me look through the microscope. Even to my untrained eye it looked as though there were few intact cells to count! Even without the microscope I could see that the culture medium, originally a clear solution, was now heavily clouded. Dr. Kmetz was further astounded because, he said, the dead cells were from a young culture and normally young cells adhere especially tightly to the bottom of the culture flask.

In a third day of tests I again quadrupled the number of floating cells in the experimental culture. My interest lay in trying to understand how I affected the cells, but when I questioned Kmetz about this he didn't know what to say to me. Taking one of the control flasks, he threw it against the wall to see if I might have affected the cells through vibration, but as in earlier tests the cells were not affected. I asked him whether there were any other ways to produce floaters, and he said that the cells could be digested off the flask with an enzyme, but that he knew of no way to produce the explosive effect I'd had on the cells.

I had been really pushing myself during this trip, and I wasn't feeling well. By the end of the third day of experiments I had developed a stomach virus and couldn't hold down any food. I fought all that night to combat whatever virus attacked, but it soon became clear that my illness would have to run its course. Sadly I called Dr. Kmetz and told him I wouldn't be able to complete the two remaining days of research. The next morning Rochelle and I went home. But I left San Antonio with a marvelous last bit of information from Dr. Kmetz: There was an infinitesimal chance—approximately .000001 in a million—of my accomplishing the destruction of the cells.

Dr. Kmetz prepared a report on the experiment,

and he stood up for the results he had witnessed first-hand in a variety of press interviews. The results of the HeLa experiment generated excitement throughout the field of parapsychology and in the popular media. In its October 3, 1977 issue, the AMA-supported journal, *The Hospital Tribune,* distributed only in hospitals, mentioned the experiment quite favorably. I was told that I was the first psychic healer ever to be written up in the journal in a favorable light. The reporter seemed to fully understand the ramifications of the cancer study.

Soon I was contacted by Harry Lynn, news director at NBC-TV in New York, about doing a three-part series on my cancer work and experiments for the evening news. I cooperated fully with them, and Harry, newscaster Melba Toliver, a camera crew, Rochelle, and I spent many hours filming discussions of the HeLa cancer cell experiment. Several clients agreed to be interviewed. I demonstrated my technique on Melba Toliver. Harry Lynn wrote to Dr. Kmetz asking for pictures representative of the cancer cells I had worked on, and Dr. Kmetz supplied a photo of intact cancer cells and a photo of scattered cellular debris.

Everyone involved was enthusiastic about the project. I was happy that the cancer experiment was being covered by a well-regarded news team, and the information I provided for the show was very well documented. Then NBC's legal department got involved. They didn't want to subject the station to the controversy that would, they felt, surround such an experiment. Harry Lynn protested NBC's censorship, which disregarded the available scientific documentation of what I'd accomplished. Ultimately only a one-line mention of the cancer experiment was made when the piece about me was aired.

Harry told me that he'd fought long and hard to overturn the decision to ignore proof that psychic healing is beneficial. He explained that showing my work in a more spiritual or religious context would have been more acceptable to the censors. And indeed, the single short segment of the evening news that was finally devoted to my work was filled with heavy religious overtones. I was made to seem like a spiritually oriented healer, rather than a scientifically oriented healer trying to validate his claims. One of my clients—of the six or seven who had been interviewed—was featured. She spoke mostly about her gratitude for my help and called me "a saint." I cringed when I heard it.

Though the news spot portrayed me in a favorable light, the religious approach stood for everything I'd been fighting against for years. Once again I was lumped in with the nonscientific side of healing. In a later conversation Harry Lynn implied that concern over job security had led to the suppression of the cancer experiment story. The NBC staff didn't want to assume responsibility for reporting a fantastic scientific discovery that dealt not only with psychic healing but with the most dreaded of modern diseases, cancer.

But the truth was not suppressed for long. Medical journalist Judith Glassman covered my work in an article, "Cancer Treatments Doctors Ignore—They Work!" which was published in *Penthouse Forum* and reprinted in the August-September 1978 issue of *Cancer News Journal*. Then, in October 1978, Michael Brown wrote a piece on parapsychology,

"Getting Serious About the Occult," for the prestigious *Atlantic Monthly* magazine. He covered many of my successful experiments and wrote very favorably about my research work. Brown, a diligent and well-respected investigative reporter, had previously published a book, *PK: A Report on Psychokinesis*, in which he had included my experiences, and has since authored *Laying Waste: The Poisoning of America by Toxic Chemicals*.

In September 1979 Albert Z. Freedman, editor of *Penthouse Forum*, hired Judith Glassman to write an extensive article about my healing abilities. I was given the opportunity to see a copy of the article before it went to press, and as I read it, I wondered what scientists would say when they read or heard about Dr. Kmetz's quotes on the HeLa experiment. "He blew those cells apart," Dr. Kmetz was quoted as saying. "After he worked on them the flask was full of cellular debris, bits and pieces of cells rather than whole cells." Acknowledging that he had worked with other sensitives and psychics, Dr. Kmetz said, "Nothing has been quite as dramatic as Dean."

I wondered how the skeptics would write that off. I half expected a scientist to advance the theory that cells in a test tube could be hypnotized to destroy themselves! But Dr. Kmetz's candidness with the press, so different from what I was used to, made all the difficulties I'd encountered previously with the scientific community seem worthwhile. I only hoped the experiment would lead more doctors and scientists to realize the importance of further investigation of psychic healing and its possible use as an adjunct to traditional medicine.

Sometimes my life seems like a journey through an

unmapped terrain: I'm always wondering where the next turn in the path is going to take me. But as I look back over the years since I got the first inkling of my paranormal abilities in Buddy Geier's rented car, I see that I've devoted myself to two major endeavors: healing and scientific research.

In the beginning I was very defensive about my healing career, and my interest in research was fueled by my desire for credibility and acceptance. Now I pursue the scientific question out of curiosity, and in the hopes that my "power," once understood, may someday be taught or even synthesized. But I'm no longer driven by the need to prove myself.

I still believe that there's a need for more doctors and scientists to open their minds and start doing research into psychic healing. But the world resists change, and all parapsychology researchers are headed uphill against the wind.

The general public and the majority of scientists don't yet accept parapsychology as a legitimate science. The field is so new that scientists are groping. Most researchers can really only deal with failed experiments. If a psychic fails to perform PK, for example, the experimenter has no problem. But if a psychic does perform PK, the researcher doesn't know how to proceed. Until technology is further advanced and better experiments are developed to study and explain psychic phenomena, they just can't be judged by pure scientific methods. One cannot measure love or inspiration—at least not yet—but we all see and marvel at their manifestations. In the case of psychic healing, results can often be demonstrated, but the essence, thus far, remains as elusive as love.

For all the effort I've put into the search for scientific validation, it is always my greatest joy to return to healing. People are far more important to me than science. Working directly with my patients and seeing them get well is more rewarding to me than holding a test tube could ever be. When people start to feel better and I can see the change in their lives, the happiness I feel is everlasting, whereas the gratification of succeeding in laboratory experiments lasts only a moment. When I think of my life as a healer I like to think of Helen Titunik, who was so close to death when I met her and is now alive and well, and spreading joy with her loving and positive attitude. I like to think of Pauline Sheinis, who couldn't walk, and who now teaches needlepoint every day at a senior citizen's center. I like to think of Jennifer Paul, who as an infant was thought to be doomed to a life of deafness, but is growing up with normal hearing. The bottom line in my life is bringing health and happiness to people, even if I can't fully explain how I do it.

Afterword
by
John M. Kmetz, Ph.D.

The preceding pages have been an account of Dean Kraft's capacity to affect natural and physical systems in an unusual way. The majority of the work deals with Dean Kraft's gift as a healer. Numerous examples have been given of his power to somehow channel his energy to an affected person to effect a cure. It is noteworthy that he has not only healed people suffering from a variety of diseases, but that many of these people have been referred to him by their physicians.

The case histories of these people, both before and after treatment by Mr. Kraft, are substantive proof that he can somehow accelerate the normal healing process of the body, even in the case of cancer. Cases of spontaneous cancer remission do occur, which imply that the body has the ability to initiate cancer regression. However, our knowledge about the exact causes of cancer is far from complete, and we know even less about the process of spontaneous remission.

In an attempt to understand his ability, Dean Kraft has taken part in a number of interesting scientific experiments at respected research institutions, and has demonstrated both his ability to influence physical systems and his ability to change another person's physiological functions by a "laying on of hands." At Lawrence Livermore Laboratories in California he was able to cause cancer cells to detach and float free from the surface on which they were growing.

The cell study was subsequently repeated at Science Unlimited Research Foundation, in San Antonio, Texas, with the same results. I was at that time director of SURF and supervised the experiments. Dean Kraft consistently caused cancer cells to detach from their growing surface and float free in the culture medium, indicating that they were destroyed. Even though the results of these tests were exciting, they gave no clues concerning the nature of the energy form emanating from Dean Kraft.

This has been the story of an individual's attempts to understand not only the changes that have occurred in his life, but also to learn whether or not his healing ability can be characterized scientifically. It points to the need for more research in this area. For example, can we characterize the nature of the interaction between the healer and a patient? Can we characterize the energy involved? And finally, can individuals be trained to exhibit this ability? Only future research will give us the answers.

Appendix

The following is a report by Dr. Kmetz describing experiments in which I attempted to get HeLa cancer cells to float free of the culture flask in which they were contained. The tests were conducted at Science Unlimited Research Foundation in San Antonio, Texas, in July 1977.

SCIENCE UNLIMITED RESEARCH FOUNDATION

Cell Culture Experiments with Dean Kraft.

Introduction

This report describes procedures and results of experiments conducted with Dean Kraft, a well-known psychic healer practicing in New York City, during the period July 14, 1977, through July 16, 1977. The experiment was an attempt to replicate an experiment that he had performed earlier at Lawrence Livermore

Laboratories in California that involved his being able to get cells grown in a monolayer culture to lift free from the culture flask.

Materials and Methods

Cell Cultures: HeLa cells (Flow Laboratories, Rockville, Maryland) were maintained in 50 cc culture flasks (Falcon, Oxnard, California) with a 25 cm^2 growth area. Cells were maintained with Eagle's minimal essential medium supplemented with 10 percent fetal calf serum and 1 percent antibiotic-antimycotic solution (GIBCO, Grand Island, New York). Cultures used for experiments were 75 percent to 100 percent confluent.

Cell Counts: The number of free floating cells in the culture medium were counted using a hemacytometer (American Optical, Buffalo, New York—bright line with improved Neubauer ruling). In practice, a culture flask was randomly selected for an experiment. The flask was gently swirled to evenly distribute the free floating cells in the medium, and an aliquot of approximately 1 ml was quickly removed from the flask to a 12 × 75 mm culture tube. Replicate counts were then made from this aliquot. Cells were counted in the four corner squares of the hemacytometer (each square = 1 mm^2) and the results presented as average number of cells per mm^2. The above procedure was followed both for control cultures and cultures handled by Dean Kraft.

Treatment Procedure: Treatment by Dean Kraft consisted of Mr. Kraft entering his healing state and treating the cells for twenty minutes. During the treatment period Mr. Kraft was seated in a comfortable chair. His treatment varied from his holding the flask between his hands to simply placing it on the arm of the chair and holding his hand above the flask. All treatment sessions occurred in a 9 × 12 RF shielded room.

Results

The results are presented in Tables 1 through 6. In every session, Mr. Kraft was able to significantly increase the number of cells floating in the medium (Tables 1, 4, and 6) while the controls, consisting of a culture placed on a table for 20 minutes, or flasks held by a second individual, not having any healing ability, showed no change in the number of free floating cells during the 20-minute sessions.

Session 2 (Tables 2, 3, and 4) is somewhat of an anomaly from the others. This session was a 60-minute session to see if Mr. Kraft could continue to increase the number of free floating cells with successive treatments. The cells were counted after each 20-minute interval. As can be seen, no significant results were obtained until the final 20-minute interval. Again, the controls showed no change.

Session 3 (Table 5) did not involve treatment by Mr. Kraft. During this session the flask was vigorously shaken to demonstrate that the cells are firmly attached to the culture flask.

Visual Observations: My observations of the cells after an experimental session with Dean Kraft indicated that the cells appeared to be severely damaged. The cell suspension contained not only complete cells, but also many cell fragments. The suspension was also cloudy following a session, but was clear before the session began.

Interesting Note: After each session, before the results were analyzed, Mr. Kraft was asked his subjective impressions as to what extent if any he thought he affected the cell cultures. After analysis, Mr. Kraft's subjective impressions were accurate as to the extent of the interaction he had with the cell culture.

Conclusion

The results of these preliminary experiments with Dean Kraft indicate that he was able to substantially increase the number of free floating cells in the culture medium. They indicate that further work along this line should be performed with Mr. Kraft. If Mr. Kraft can duplicate these results in a second series, the combined results should provide a firm base upon which to structure future experiments with him in an attempt to determine just what he is changing in the cells to cause them to not only detach from the flask but become severely damaged.

Since the experiments in July several other attempts to dislodge cells from the flasks have been performed. These attempts included (1) keeping the medium off the cell for extended periods of time; and (2) placing the flasks on a vibrator for periods of time. Neither of these have proven a successful means of increasing the number of free floating cells.

John M. Kmetz, Ph. D.
October 7, 1977

Table 1

Trial—HeLa 1   7/14/77

Time (Min.) Subject	0	20	t between 0 & 20
DK	1.3 ± 1.0	6.0 ± 0.89	8.47 sig .001
JKm	1.0 ± 0.63	0.83 ± 0.75	.416 n.s.
Control	1.2 ± 1.1	1.0 ± 0.0	.338 n.s.

Cell figures are avg. # cell/mm² $\pm$ S.D.

Table 2

Trial—HeLa 2   7/15/77

Time (Min.) Subject	0	20	t between 0 & 20
DK	0.833 ± 0.753	1.66 ± 1.03	1.59 n.s.
JKi	1.16 ± 1.17	1.0 ± 0	.335 n.s.
Control	0.833 ± 0.753	1.16 ± 0.753	.753 n.s.

Table 3

Trial—HeLa 2   7/15/77

Time (Min.) Subject	0	40	t between 0 & 40
DK	0.833 ± 0.753	2.33 ± 1.86	1.83 n.s.
JKi	—	—	—
Control	0.833 ± 0.753	1.33 ± 0.516	1.33 n.s.

JKi did not participate in this session

Table 4

Trial—HeLa 2   7/15/77

Time (Min.) Subject	0	60	t between 40 & 60
DK	2.83 ± 1.47	27.33 ± 6.3	9.24 sig .001
JKi	1.83 ± 0.753	1.50 ± 0.548	0.868 n.s.
Control	1.50 ± 0.548	1.33 ± 1.03	0.357 n.s.

Cell counts are on same cultures as used for the 20- and 40-minute sessions. The 20- and 40-minute sessions were held in the morning, while the additional 20-minute session was held in the afternoon.

Table 5

Trial—HeLa 3   7/16/77

Time (Min.) Subject	0	20	t between 0 & 20
Control	1.16 ± 0.753	1.0 ± 0.632	0.399 n.s.

Trial 3 involved making an initial cell count on a culture and then shaking it vigorously, tapping it against the wall, and making the second count.

Table 6

Trial—HeLa 4   7/16/77

Time (Min.) Subject	0	20	t between 0 & 20
DK	1.17 ± 0.753	3.33 ± 0.816	4.77 sig. at .001
JKm	1.89 ± 0.782	1.33 ± 0.516	1.46 n.s.
Control	1.16 ± 0.753	1.50 ± 1.04	0.649 n.s.

EXPLORE THE FRONTIER OF PSYCHIC KNOWLEDGE

__**THE AIRMEN WHO WOULD NOT DIE** John G. Fuller	04273-1 – \$2.50
__**CHARIOTS OF THE GODS?** Erich Von Däniken	04381-9 – \$2.50
__**THE HUMAN AURA** Nicholas Regush	05321-0 – \$2.75
__**MY SEARCH FOR THE GHOST OF** **FLIGHT 401** Elizabeth Fuller	04011-9 – \$1.95
__**PHONE CALLS FROM THE DEAD** D. Scott Rogo and Raymond Bayless	04559-5 – \$2.25
__**PSYCHIC ARCHAEOLOGY** Jeffrey Goodman	05000-9 – \$2.50
__**WE ARE THE EARTHQUAKE** **GENERATION** Jeffrey Goodman	04991-4 – \$2.75
__**THE STAR PEOPLE** Brad and Francie Steiger	05513-2 – \$2.75

EDGAR CAYCE
World Renowned Psychic

MS READ-a-thon—
a simple way to start
youngsters reading

Boys and girls between 6 and 14 can join the MS READ-a-thon and help find a cure for Multiple Sclerosis by reading books. And they get two rewards — the enjoyment of reading, and the great feeling that comes from helping others.

Parents and educators: For complete information call your local MS chapter. Or mail the coupon below.

Kids can help, too!